GARLAND STUDIES IN

ENTREPRENEURSHIP

edited by

STUART BRUCHEY
UNIVERSITY OF MAINE

AFRICAN AMERICAN ENTREPRENEURSHIP IN RICHMOND, 1890–1940

THE STORY OF R.C. SCOTT

MICHAEL A. PLATER

Routledge
Taylor & Francis Group

NEW YORK AND LONDON

First published 1996 by Garland Publishing, Inc.

Published 2016 by Routledge
711 Third Avenue, New York, NY 10017
2 Park Square, Milton Park, Abingdon, Oxfordshire OX14 4RN

First issued in paperback 2016

Routledge is an imprint of the Taylor and Francis Group, an informa business

Library of Congress Cataloging-in-Publication Data

Plater, Michael A., 1956–
    African American entrepreneurship in Richmond, 1890–1940 :
the story of R.C. Scott / Michael A. Plater.
        p.   cm. — (Garland studies in entrepreneurship)
    Includes bibliographical references and index.
    ISBN 0-8153-2673-4 (alk. paper)
    1. Scott, R.C. 2. Afro-Americans in business—Biography.
3. Afro-American business enterprises—Virginia—Richmond—
History. 4. Undertakers and undertaking—Virginia—Richmond—
History. 5. Entrepreneurship—Virginia—Richmond. I. Title.
II. Series.
HD9999.U52S386 1996
338.7'6136375'09755451—dc20   96-34645

ISBN 13: 978-1-1389-8834-7 (pbk)
ISBN 13: 978-0-8153-2673-1 (hbk)

Dedication

This work is dedicated to my mother, Mrs. Veida Freeman Claytor, whose guidance and constant support inspired me throughout my educational career.

Contents

Page

Dedication..v
Table of contents..vii
List of Tables..ix
List of Illustrations..xi
Preface..xiii
Introduction..xvii
Acknowledgments...xxiii
Chapter I...3
    African American Funeral Home Directors in Richmond
Chapter II..41
    The History of Funeral Directing in America
Chapter III...83
    The Origin of African American Death and Mourning Rituals
Chapter IV...107
    Folk Beliefs and Current Practices
Chapter V..127
    African American Insurance Enterprises
Chapter VI...151
    The Funeral of Brother Jesse Harding
Chapter VII..161
    Conclusion
Appendix A..167
    Richmond Data Analysis
Bibliography..177
Index..189

List of Tables

Table   Page

1. State Embalming Requirements, 1926.........................53

2. Growth of the Manufacture and Wholesale Value of Burial Goods, 1859-1925.......................................60

3. Distribution of Estates, New York and Kings Counties, 1926..64

4. Distribution of New York County Estates by Size, 1926..66

5. "Extra" Charges in Various New York County Estates, 1926..67

6. Burial Expenses in "Net" Funeral Bill of Estates in New York County, 1926...70

7. Distribution of Estates by Size and Average Funeral Bill, Cook County, Illinois, 1926..............................73

8. Average Amounts Claimed and Allowed for Funeral Expenses, Cook County, Illinois, 1926.......................74

9. Approved and Contested Undertakers' Bills, Cook County, Illinois, 1926..75

10. Adult Funeral Cost for 7,871 Industrial Policyholders By States, 1927..78

11. Adult Funeral Cost for 2,765 Industrial Policyholders, By Cities, 1927..79

12.   Funeral Cost for 957 Children Under Twelve. 1927......80

13.   A Speculative Geographical Distribution of Slave
       Imports During the Whole Period of the Atlantic
       Slave Trade...92

14.   Slave Imported into the North American Mainland,
       by Origin...97

15.   Insurance in Force for Various Countries, 1935-38......129

16.   Rates of the Prudential Insurance Company of
       America, 1881..136

17.   Repossessed African American Fraternal Buildings,
       by States, 1940...141

18.   The True Reformers' Class Department Rate Table,
       1885..143

List of Illustrations

Illustration   Page

1.   A. D. Price Funeral Home Complex, Early Twentieth
      Century (1)..10

2.   A. D. Price Funeral Home Complex, Early Twentieth
      Century (2)..11

3.   Fisk Metallic Burial Case, 1848, Patent Sketch 43

4.   Corpse Cooler of Frederick and Trump, 1846...............45

5.   Estimates of the U.S. Population, 1900-1940...............50

6.   Estimates of U.S. Deaths, 1900-1940........................50

7.   Annual Deaths per Funeral Home, 1900-1940..............51

8.   Distribution of Slave Imports...................................91

Preface

On February 11, 1993, relatives buried Arthur Ashe at Woodland Cemetery in Richmond, Virginia. *The Washington Post* described this historically African American cemetery as a "dumping ground for appliances, tires, and other trash" and ten weeks after the funeral they noted "dandelions are springing up in the uncut grass around Ashe's grave" (*The Washington Post* 1993, 30 April). Arthur Ashe, the first African American man to win the Wimbledon tennis championship, requested burial in this cemetery to highlight the social conditions of African Americans in Richmond. His grave site provides a visual image of the decline of many financial, economic, and cultural institutions built by African Americans in the early twentieth-century.

Until 1970, the privately-owned cemeteries of Woodland and Evergreen were the only places available for African American burials in Richmond. The city-operated cemeteries remained segregated until well over a century after slaves became free in America (*The Washington Post* 1993, 30 April). These two cemeteries were the pride of the African American community for nearly one hundred years. John Mitchell, city council member and editor of the *Richmond Planet*, was a president of the Woodland Cemetery, and funeral director A. D. Price served as the president of Evergreen Cemetery from 1917 until his death in 1921. However, as the African American community gained greater burial options after 1970, these venerated institutions declined into the wretched state observed at the time of Arthur Ashe's burial. Ashe's decision to join John Jasper, Maggie Walker, and others at Woodland Cemetery was a tribute to the past leaders and institutions of Richmond's African American community.

The vitality of Woodland and Evergreen cemeteries in the Richmond Community depended on their segregated status. During the turn of the century, these cemeteries, along with many other social organizations, businesses, and institutions, formed a circulatory system in the community. This system kept the Richmond African American community alive and warded off the deplorable conditions imposed by racism.

This book proposes to look at the economic center of this circulatory system and develop a pattern of analysis to investigate similar systems in the early twentieth-century. The book argues that the funeral industry was the economic center and uses the funeral director as the model for African American entrepreneurship during the study period.

I believe this book contributes to the scholarly conversation about African American business in Southern cities, the role of business in African American urban society, and the issues of class and social relations within African American communities in the following four areas.

1)   Previous investigations on early African American entrepreneurship centered on individual entrepreneurs and the special circumstances surrounding their success. This study defines successful African American entrepreneurial traits and argues that each community had one or more individuals exhibiting these traits. The individuals possessing these traits gained elite status in both the African American and white communities of their respective cities. By looking at an industry and a set of entrepreneurial traits that were present in all communities, this analysis provides a system to compare entrepreneurs, elite status, and race relations across communities.

2)   The current studies of business history typically focus on organizational accomplishments, managerial evolution, and the impact of politics, regulation, or leadership changes on the organization. This book analyzes business history through the lens of culture. I define the funeral home industry as a cultural phenomenon. I assert that researchers must view all early twentieth-century industries in the African American community through cultural context, if they want to measure the flow of power and influence.

3)   The enclave theory when applied to the funeral industry provides an economic model to validate the correlation between a strong African American funeral industry and the community's economic strength. This book presents the foundation for this correlation.

4)   This work directly challenges the notion that economic risk-taking was absent or not rewarded in the African American community. I prove that innovation was a driving force in the African American funeral industry. Richmond's African American funeral directors embraced innovations at such a rapid pace that they far outdistanced their white counterparts.

The funeral industry operated on a voluntarily segregated basis. This structure provided valuable economic opportunities for African American entrepreneurs. The structure also provides a way to compare economic development between races and different cities. The book makes these arguments by researching the lives of Richmond funeral directors R. C. Scott and A. D. Price. Their account illustrates the interconnection of African American business to the internal social and economic services provided to the community.

Introduction

This study examines the socioeconomic aspects of ethnicity as a way to understand African American entrepreneurship in the early twentieth century. Researchers cannot understand early twentieth-century African American entrepreneurship simply by investigating business success factors such as the available capital, location, or labor structure. These factors fail to reveal the influence of culture and the environment on entrepreneurial success. I believe to accurately investigate early twentieth-century African American entrepreneurship, one must separate the influence of ethnicity from the social and environmental elements that restrained its efforts.

I achieve this separation of culture and environment by researching the African American funeral home industry. The funeral industry provides a rare example of an industry that successfully operated under the separate but equal doctrine, and had the absolute consent of most ethnic groups. Funeral service was a profitable industry that African Americans engaged in without white competition. Yet, while the industry segregated clients, new technology and services flowed across racial boundaries, limited only by economic constraints.

Traditionally, scholars concentrate on individuals when studying African American entrepreneurship (Walker 1986, 343-382; Henderson 1987, 216-242; Schweninger 1989, 22-60; Kenzer 1989, 61-87). However, this conventional approach usually emphasizes the unique circumstances that provided entrepreneurial opportunities. Highlighting opportunities tied to a specific time, place, and set of circumstances does not illustrate the more general African American entrepreneurial characteristics. In contrast, I propose to analyze an industry that existed in nearly all African American communities. Success and failure of this industry, in these communities, depended on entrepreneurial traits and the industry structure, not special circumstances. In most cities, a small subset of the funeral directors belonged to the business elite. By identifying the entrepreneurial traits present in these elite funeral directors, this study will introduce a more comprehensive approach to understanding the African American value system and how that value system encouraged entrepreneurial success.

The funeral industry redistributed tremendous amounts of capital in the African American community. Because funeral service was a church-sanctioned ritual and the industry had enormous economic influence in the community, I contend that funeral directors were major power brokers in early twentieth-century African American communities. My assertion that funeral directors were the major power brokers is contrary to the intuitive perception that preachers, lawyers, and physicians dominated the community business and elite social circles. This study examines economic power and community status to reveal another power structure within the African American community.

CONCEPTS FOR THE STUDY

The concepts framing this study revolve around the debate between Booker T. Washington and W. E. B. Du Bois over segregation and assimilation, and the ethnic enclave theory: a theoretical model of economic structures in minority communities. Within this framework, the study employs an interdisciplinary approach to define both the business success factors and the critical cultural-based community environment.

Du Bois versus Washington

The interest and even fascination with which the Negro people have always viewed the great mystery of death has given the ceremonies that are connected with this dread event a special and peculiarly important place in their social life. Out of this instinctive awe and reverence for the dead has arisen the demand for solemn and decent and often elaborate burial services. To meet this demand there has grown up a prosperous business. It is a curious fact that with the exception of that of caterer there is no business in which Negroes seem to be more numerously engaged or one in which they have been more uniformly successful. (Washington 1907, 94)

There are four undertaking establishments, two of which are conducted by women . . . They are all old establishments--six to thirty-three years--and in no branch of business, save one, has the Negro evinced so much push, taste and enterprise. Two of the establishments will, in equipment, compare favorably with the white businesses in the city. (Du Bois 1899, 118)

While Du Bois suggested the creation of an African American economic organization in 1899 (Butler and Wilson 1990, 34), Washington became known as the most vocal advocate for technocratic African American nationalism.

> Washington hoped to build a business and industrial technocracy among black people. He hoped that by responding to the demands of the age for skilled industrial workers and competent businessmen, black Americans could make themselves sophisticated contributors to the new industrial revolution. (Moses 1978, 28)

Despite the accepted interpretation of Booker T. Washington and Frederick Douglass as advocates of political African American unity and economic assimilation (Moses 1978, 96) and contrary to the intuitive perception that preachers, lawyers, and physicians dominated the community business and elite social circles, this study examines economic power and community status to reveal another power structure within the African American community. Both looked at economic development in the same way they looked at industrial education.

> Separate institutions might, in some cases, be consciousable as temporary measures while the freedmen were adjusting to their new state and developing confidence and strength. (Moses 1978, 90)

Washington understood the economic benefits of a captured African American market that African American entrepreneurs primarily supplied. He believed freedom came from economic stability and his "captains of industry" would become equal to white businesspeople in the economy. At the point of economic equality, the need for technocratic African American nationalism would no longer exist. Washington's National Negro Business League was a vehicle to encourage the growth of entrepreneurial activities in the African American community. Unfortunately, Washington's compromise on civil rights allowed Du Bois, and later the NAACP, to destroy his economic message. Du Bois looked at the segregation and the disenfranchisement advocated by Washington and saw the radical destruction of democracy and African American constitutional rights. Washington also saw this but felt a captured economic market could eventually give African Americans the power to obtain democratic privileges. By controlling significant capital resources, they could demand and receive the privileges of democracy and capitalism (Butler 1991, 64). As the integrationists led by Du Bois and the NAACP gained stature and attempted to achieve equal rights through the court systems, most African American businesses suffered. Social integration did not mean economic integration for African American businesses. The courts could not force whites to patronize their businesses and their existing African American client base deserted them to shop at white establishments.

Within the context of the Du Bois and Washington debate, the advantages of studying the funeral industry become more pronounced. While society imposed its own constraints on African American entrepreneurs because of race, this internal African American debate further weakened African American businesses by encouraging their existing client base to shop elsewhere. As a segregated industry with loyal African American clients, the funeral industry had a consistent profile throughout the early twentieth-century. Curiously, their profile and business philosophy parallel the doctrine advocated by Booker T. Washington. Therefore, analyzing the funeral industry provides a new dimension to examine the conflict between Du Bois and Washington.

Ethnic Enclave Theory

The ethnic enclave theory applies a labor market analysis to ethnic communities. The theory attempts to model economic flows within ethnic communities. Kenneth L. Wilson, a strong advocate of this theory, suggests that the key structural feature of an enclave is the interdependency among the minority-owned businesses (Wilson and Martin 1982, 135-160; Wilson and Portes 1980, 295-319; Butler and Wilson 1990, 26-27). An ethnic enclave is a distinctive economic unit built around a captured consumer market that operates as a sub-economy of the larger general economy. Entrepreneurs create many minority-owned businesses within the enclave to serve the enclave's residents or the general population. The theory measures the community's economic vitality by the level of interdependency among the minority-owned businesses. Firms are interdependent when they rely on other minority businesses within the enclave for their supplies and sell most of their products to customers within the enclave. Wilson's central hypothesis is:

> if the economic structure of a minority community develops
> in the direction of greater interdependency and self-
> sufficiency, then employment opportunities for the members
> of that community will expand and the various forms of
> income related to the minority economy will increase. (Butler
> and Wilson 1990, 1)

The longer each individual dollar circulates within the enclave, the higher
the interdependency and the higher the multiplier; a small purchase
multiplies into a much larger aggregate purchase. The increased circulation
triggers economic development.

A major reason the funeral industry achieved its high status is the
large multiplier it created in the community. Commercially, the funeral
home was the funnel for most life insurance money entering the
community. Culturally, the community's desire for proper burials created
a bond that connected the church, banking industry, and insurance industry
together. The African American funeral industry's ability to interconnect
so many aspects of the community's daily activities gave the industry its
economic and social status.

OUTLINE OF THE STUDY

The study begins with a case study of the Richmond African
American funeral home industry by featuring two firms and their founders.
The account of the A. D. Price funeral home relies on a forty-year review
of *The Richmond Planet* newspaper and a series of interviews with senior
Richmond funeral directors. A previously unpublished autobiography,
reprinted here, furnished the information for the R. C. Scott funeral home.
The history of these two men, especially R. C. Scott, establishes the
community value system, cultural environment, and social status of African
American funeral directors in the early twentieth century. The remaining
chapters explain how these values and cultural environments developed,
and how one profession successfully operated within these social
boundaries. The chapters reaffirm and provide character to R. C. Scott's
autobiography.

Chapter II traces the history of funeral service. The chapter
explores the transition of funeral service from a trade to a profession and
how the development of the European industry differed from the United
States. The chapter reviews how demographic changes in the early
twentieth century changed the industry's structure. In addition, the chapter

examines the issue of whether the poor pay a disproportionate amount for funeral expenses.

Chapter III and chapter IV investigate reasons why African American death customs might be unique. African survivals and folk beliefs contribute to our understanding of why this industry holds a special niche in the African American community. Chapter V analyzes the African American insurance industry, an industry that developed in support of the funeral industry. This chapter not only establishes the volume of insurance dollars flowing into the community through funeral directors, but illustrates the interdependency of the funeral industry with other African American institutions. The account of Jesse Harding's funeral in the last chapter exemplifies the interlocking relations surrounding death rituals in the African American community, the introduction of innovations, and how these events affected the community's everyday members.

Together these chapters depict how African American entrepreneurs developed this industry and exploited the special status granted to them by the community. Funerals, funeral processions and public ceremonies are political acts. They have practical objectives and tangible results. They are rituals used by the community for building, maintaining, and confronting power relations (Davis 1986, 5). Therefore, identifying funeral directors as power brokers in the African American community is less a recognition of their economic power than a salute to their political and social stature.

Acknowledgments

I want to express my appreciation to Chandos Brown for his patient guidance and criticism throughout the investigation. Members of the American Studies faculty at the College of William and Mary were gracious with their support, especially Richard John. The author is also indebted to Robert Gross, William Hausman, Ronald Sims, and Robert Horton for their careful reading and criticism of the manuscript in its final form.

I received critical support from the administration and faculty of the School of Business Administration at the College of William and Mary. I extend a special appreciation to John Jamison whose support of this project was unwavering. On the Business School faculty, Don Rahtz, Larry Ring, William Stewart, Hector Guerrero, Robert Johnson, Richard Flood, James Haltiner, James Olver, and Todd Mooradian were especially generous with their insights and counsel.

Portions of this book were presented to the Committee on Comparative and Historical Research on Market Economies at the University of Michigan as part of their economic history seminar series. I am grateful to the attendee's comments and the insights delivered by Margaret Levenstein.

Many individuals in the Richmond community influenced my writing. The most important members were the late John Tyson, Librarian for the State of Virginia; the late Anthony Binga from the R.C. Scott Funeral Home; and Reginald Dyson from the A. D. Price Funeral Home. I also extend my thanks to Ms. Anthony Binga and to Ms. Elaine Nichols of the South Carolina State Museum for taking time out of their schedules to talk with me.

I am intellectually indebted to my brother, James Bullock, whose probing research into my areas and sharp debates helped defined this book. His personal devotion to the cause was a great motivational factor.

In her role as a friend, co-worker, fellow student, and editor, I offer my deep appreciation to Teresa Nugent. Her help, encouragement, and criticism since the beginning of this project established a great foundation for each chapter.

However, I reserve my greatest thanks for my wife, Cassandra, and our two children, Michael Andre II and Allister Pilar, who allowed me to steal the time from our home to pursue this undertaking. I hope the completion of this document will provide inspiration for my children and a normal lifestyle for my wife.

African American Entrepreneurship in Richmond, 1890–1940

I
African American Funeral Home Directors In Richmond

INTRODUCTION

This study uses the personal stories of two prominent individuals to examine African American funeral service in Richmond. The cultural and professional practices illustrated in the narratives about A. D. Price, Sr. (1860-1921) and R. C. Scott, Sr. (1888-1957) creates the foundation for analyzing this industry in Richmond.

Two primary sources form the basis for the personal history of A. D. Price: the *Richmond Planet* (the leading African American weekly newspaper); and a series of interviews with Reginald Dyson from A. D. Price funeral home and the late Anthony Binga from R. C. Scott funeral home. A. D. Price funeral home is the oldest African American funeral home in Richmond. While A. D. Price, Sr. started several other businesses before entering the undertaking trade in 1886, this enterprise eventually dominated his commercial activities. By the early twentieth century, the African American press considered A. D. Price, Sr. "the leading undertaker of Richmond" (*Richmond Planet* 1916, 22 April), and they touted his inventory of equipment as the best in the South (*Southern Aid Messenger* 1908). A. D. Price was a prominent role model for the younger R. C. Scott. Price elevated himself into Richmond's business elite through his commitment to community service and economic prowess. Price and his arch rival W. I. Johnson secured the prominence later enjoyed by most funeral directors within the Richmond community. R. C. Scott was an aggressive member of the progressive second generation of Richmond funeral directors and eventually achieved the elite status of his elder role models.

The final section of this chapter presents the history of R. C. Scott in his own words. Robert Crafton Scott dictated this previously unpublished autobiography to Anthony J. Binga, his son-in-law, between 1953 and 1957. While all the statements cannot be independently confirmed, the value of this section is the insight it offers into an African American funeral director's view of his business and civic obligations.

3

THE RICHMOND BUSINESS COMUNITY

Various economic and geographic circumstances shaped
Richmond's postwar decline, but Richmond stagnated chiefly
because its leaders did not want nineteenth-century material
progress, not badly enough, not with the alien things that
accompanied it. The New South creed held that industry and
scientific agriculture promise progress-prosperity, sectional
reconciliation, and racial harmony-but it was a progress in
which Richmond chose not fully to participate in. Many
Richmonders thought they could have both the Old South and
the New, both the Lost Cause and the American dream.
They made Richmond the old city of the New South. They
preferred, perhaps without knowing it, the familiar cadence
of decline. Tradition and the past were more powerful or
attractive than progress. Beneficial at times, more often
destructive, the city's enduring conservatism was the
essential characteristic of Richmond after the war. (Chesson
1981, xv)

Despite the destruction from the Civil War, Richmond had the
infrastructure for Southern commercial dominance. By 1923 Richmond
had several industries (woodwork, baking powder, flour, blotting paper,
bottled extract, locomotive, fertilizer, and tobacco) that were the largest in
the world. Durham was a distant second in the volume of cigarettes and
cigars produced. In the South, Richmond boasted the largest insurance
company, paper bag manufacturer, automobile jobbers' supply house,
engraving plant, lithographing establishment, chewing gum factory, and
mail order service (Gavins 1977, 41). Yet, Richmond failed to reach its
potential because the city refused to incorporate innovations or embrace
new relationships with the North and its own African American
community. Instead, Richmond devoted a significant amount of energy
trying to recreate their previous lifestyle and ways of conducting business.
Richmond's business leaders were conservative and unabashed
believers in white superiority. While some Democratic party bosses and
cultured patricians wielded power at the highest level, "all members of the
elite were uniformly paternalistic on the Negro question . . . and shunned
the company of liberals in the Interracial Commission" (Gavins 1977, 42).
The restoration of white hegemony in social and political relations was a

constant goal of the Richmond business elite. They used city planning to regulate the residential patterns of the city, disfranchisement to preempt the politics of race, and economics to thwart threats to the white capital structure.

> In Richmond between 1885 and 1915 all blacks were removed from the city council; the only predominantly black political district, Jackson Ward, was gerrymandered out of existence; the state constitutional convention disfranchised the majority of black Virginians; first the railroads and streetcars and later the jail, juries, and neighborhoods were segregated; black principals were removed from the public schools and the right of blacks to teach was questioned; the state legislature decided to substitute white for black control of Virginia Normal and College and to strike "and College" from both name and function; and numerous other restrictions were imposed. (Brown 1989, 627)

When Maggie Walker and the Independent Order of Saint Luke opened a department store in 1905 that catered to the African American community, white merchants harassed the establishment until the store went out of business. A white retail dealer's association formed specifically to crush the store (Brown 1989, 625). They opposed the store because any dollars spent at the St. Luke Emporium would come out of their pockets.

Despite Richmond's hostile racial climate, African American businesses survived. In 1889, the city had five African American doctors, four lawyers and a dentist (Chesson 1981, 195). By 1921, African American professionals composed one of the city's twenty-three architects, twelve of two hundred and seventy-three lawyers, thirteen of four hundred and twelve notaries, seven of ninety-nine dentists, one of twenty opticians, fifteen of two hundred and thirty-three registered nurses, and twenty-four of two hundred and sixty-eight doctors. Besides these professionals, Richmond's African American community boasted a profusion of small establishments (135 barber and beauty shops, 20 clubs and pool halls, 72 dry cleaners and laundries, 33 coal and wood dealers, 55 dressmakers, 57 eating houses, 17 fish markets, 51 shoe repairpeople, 43 courier services, and 139 retail grocers). However, the organizations that controlled the flow of capital in Richmond's African American community were the four banks, three newspapers, fourteen funeral homes, five theaters, sixty-five churches, nine insurance companies, and many mutual benefit societies (Gavins 1977, 45). A common factor among these major creators of community capital was their reliance on African American clients. Each was separate from the white business structure and non-threatening to the white elite. Except the theaters and newspapers, the funeral business was a major part of each of the other businesses. By 1889, African Americans already composed half Richmond's funeral directors. A look at the leading funeral home directors is an excellent way to observe the African American economic elite and capital flows in the Richmond African American community.

Richmond's conservative democratic elite persecuted all of the city's republicans whatever their race. African American leaders either resided in the conservative wing of the republican party or avoided politics totally (Chesson 1981, 97). Businesspeople and ministers were especially vulnerable. Their power depended on balancing what was a favorable stance to the white power elite and what was acceptable to their African American constituents. While a congregation could pressure their minister to pursue a more aggressive stance on social conditions, the African American community expected very conservative, non-political behavior from their funeral directors. Thus, funeral directors were free to broker economic and behind-the-scene political power between the white elite and the African American community. Both segments of Richmond society universally accepted them because of their non-controversial demeanor, conservative practices, business acumen, and religious-based economic strength.

A. D. PRICE

> If a man die, shall he live again, is not half so important to some people as is, if a man die, will he be buried properly? Funeral Director A. D. Price will answer that question [Newspaper Ad] (*Richmond Planet* 1916, 3 June).

A. D. Price was born near Ashland, Virginia in Hanover County on August 9, 1860. Even at an early age, he enjoyed the risk associated with business enterprises. He was the consummate entrepreneur. Price only attended public school for a few years. At age seven, he left home to work in Richmond. He soon returned to Hanover and clerked for his mother in their country variety store. Motivated to expand his set of opportunities, he obtained an apprenticeship in the blacksmith trade in 1874. At age fourteen, the apprenticeship gave Price the opportunity to earn forty dollars a year while mastering a transferable skill. Upon completing his apprenticeship in 1877, he secured a blacksmith position in Richmond. Within a year, he was master of his trade and working his own forge. Using the money he saved from his blacksmith work, Price opened a small brokerage business as his first entrepreneurial venture. This first business venture subsequently failed. While unsuccessful in the brokerage business, Price still had enough remaining capital to start his own blacksmith and wheelwright business in 1881. Even after outfitting this enterprise, he had the resources to put away $150 "to tramp with in case of further failure" (*Southern Aid Messenger* 1908). In contrast to the first business, this enterprise relied on his learned trade and grew tremendously. He employed both African American and white mechanics to sustain the growth (*Southern Aid Messenger* 1908).

Price recognized early the movement toward consolidated funeral activities. During the late nineteenth century, many trades that conducted isolated undertaking services (sexton, cabinetmaker, liveryperson etc.) began converging into a separate undertaking trade (Habenstein and Lamers 1955, 231). In 1886, Price added undertaking and livery services to his establishment. After a rocky beginning, the undertaking business prospered with his extensive livery as a foundation. By 1908, this livery included the following inventory:

> ...twenty-five first-class rubber-tired carriages, four late style funeral cars, two massive undertaking wagons, (one of which was the finest in the State), two latest style undertaking buggies, pleasure wagons, omnibuses and vehicles of nearly every kind usual for a first-class up-to-date livery business (*Southern Aid Messenger* 1908).

Many Richmond African Americans were without personal transportation in this period. A. D. Price interceded and supplied the community's requirements. He provided delivery equipment for other businesses, wagons for moving, and carriages for courting. Since Price had the finest horses and the most elaborate carriages, the A. D. Price funeral home became an integral part of the Richmond courting scene. Hiring an elaborate hack and a beautiful pair of horses from Mr. Price was the ultimate Sunday courting ritual. This Sunday excursion was the ideal way for a man publicly to display his adoration for his lady (Binga 1989). His range of services gave Price an advantage in securing clients.   He attempted to use that advantage in the following *Richmond Planet* advertisements:

> A. D. Price declares that he leads. No one will deny him in this respect. He will lead you either to the bridal altar or to the grave yard and he will give you absolute satisfaction in either of these places. His livery is kept up to the minute and his automobile service is the very best. If you are happy, call and see him.   If you are sad go to him with your troubles. His terms are as low as any, commensurate with first class service (*Richmond Planet* 1916, 16 December).

> You don't have to die in order to find out the kind of service you will get at a Price funeral.   Prompt attention to all orders. If you wish to enjoy yourself, get married and be satisfied. Then you'll be sure to leave instructions as to the disposition of your remains at death (*Richmond Planet* 1916, 29 July).

At one point before the conversion to motor equipment, Price had between 36 and 40 work horses in his stables (Dyson 1989B, Binga 1989, *Southern Aid Messenger* 1908). While other African American funeral homes rented hacks and horses to the community, Price had the largest number of funeral carriages among African American and white funeral directors (Dyson 1989A).   In addition, Richmond's African American funeral directors as a group had more equipment than Richmond's white funeral directors.

> A prominent white gentleman informed us last Wednesday that the funeral of a prominent white person had to be postponed a few days before because of the inability to secure enough carriages for the mourners and their friends. In talking with a white funeral director, he had been informed that the colored undertakers owned more carriages than all of the white undertakers combined and that the latter were in a large measure dependent upon them whenever they had a large order to fill. (*Richmond Planet* 1908, 2 May)

Price enhanced his status and power in the city by maintaining a large inventory of funeral apparatus and furnishings. He became the supplier for many smaller funeral homes, which, consequently, had to arrange their funerals around the availability of Price's equipment.

Race remained a barrier in most other African American businesses; however, funeral equipment and supplies routinely crossed racial lines. Despite the public's insistence on segregated funeral homes, funeral equipment and supplies were completely transferable among various ethnic funerals. If a funeral home needed a casket that it did not have in stock, it did not matter whether the funeral home with the item was African American or white. According to Reginald Dyson from A. D. Price funeral home and Anthony Binga from R. C. Scott funeral home, behind the public facade there was tremendous rapport across racial lines. Funeral directors exchanged supplies and equipment based on reputation and reliability, not race. The *Richmond Planet* confirmed these exchanges in an article printed on February 2, 1902 about a loaded hearse that crashed. A pair of horses slid on a patch of ice and overturned the hearse, smashed the glass and disarranged the coffin. The article notes that the hearse used by Funeral Director Brown, a small African American funeral home, belonged to Joseph Bliley, a leading white funeral home at the time (*Richmond Planet* 1902, 2 February). In this cooperative, behind-the-scene environment, the A. D. Price funeral home played a very influential role.

After five very productive years (1893-1898) at 412 and 414 North Third Street, Price amassed enough capital to begin building a complex of structures in Richmond's Jackson Ward. He purchased lots at 210 and 212 East Leigh Street and initially constructed a three-story, five-bay, brick structure (Illustration 1). The building was 30 feet across the front and had a 150-feet depth. In this first building Price initially conducted all of his undertaking, embalming, and livery businesses. Price deliberately designed the three-story building so all funeral and livery activities were on the first floor of the structure. The top two floors held many elaborately decorated halls and rooms. Organizations and individuals rented these chambers for public and private entertainment. The lodges also used them as meeting places (*Southern Aid Messenger* 1908). The lodges were affiliates of the secret societies and fraternal orders that provided most of the social activities beyond the family and church. When Reginald Dyson joined A. D. Price funeral home in 1931 at the age of fourteen, he did not start in the funeral component of the business. He started by working for Mrs. Price and caring for the funeral home's top

Illustration 1
A.D. Price Funeral Home Complex
Early Twentieth Century
Dementi Foster Studios, Richmond

Illustration 2
A.D. Price Funeral Home Complex
Early Twentieth Century
Dementi Foster Studios, Richmond

two floors. These floors contained fourteen meeting rooms that Mrs. Price, a former Fisk Jubilee singer, rented out. Whether used by the public or secret societies, the rooms always had groups in them (Dyson 1989A). Immediately to the left of the funeral home building (facing the building from the street), a small two-story dwelling housed the business office and served as A. D. Price's home (Illustration 1).

In 1912, Price built a three-story, three-bay apartment building to the left of his home. A. D. Price Jr. lived in the second floor flat of this apartment building. In illustration 2, Price Jr.'s apartment is the one with the enclosed porch. The son eventually took over the business from his father, Price Sr. Today, this former apartment building is the current A. D. Price funeral home. Directly behind the apartment building is a two-story, five-bay structure built between 1901 and 1914 to store equipment and serve as a stable. Price installed a manual counterbalanced elevator in the building. This device allowed two people to hoist twenty-five hundred pound carriages to the second floor for storage.

A. D. Price designed the buildings in the Price complex on Leigh street to reflect his priorities and role in the community. Despite his success in the undertaking, embalming and livery businesses, he limited these activities to only one third of the space in his first structure. Within the Richmond African American community there was significant demand for meeting space, but few African Americans controlled such spaces. A vast network of fraternal societies needed places to meet, yet churches prohibited activities such as card playing, drinking, gambling, and dancing from taking place within their doors. The funeral profession fulfilled this need by personally shouldering the cost of providing facilities for community organizations. While the community preferred this arrangement for many reasons, a primary reason was price. By providing meeting space, the funeral profession also strengthened the economic base of the community's social organizations. These organizations could forego building their own spaces or paying exorbitant fees for meeting space. Funeral Directors charged nominal fees because they viewed these rental activities as part of their regular business services and community outreach.

The activities conducted in Price's hall were numerous and diverse. On December 4, 1899, the Pure Gold Court gave a Bazaar at Price's hall for the benefit of the Richmond Lodge. The Secret Sons of Love under the leadership of W. I. Johnson [the funeral director] held another bazaar at Price's hall the week before. A joint excursion composed of the Rescue Steam Fire Department No. 1, Ready and Willing Hand and Ladder Co., and the Brighton, and Cannon Hand Engine Co., 3, also used Price's hall:

> We have secured one of the largest Halls in Richmond for
> the accommodation of the many friends that are with us. We
> will also have a presentation of a gold medal, which will be
> presented to the Chief Engineer, James Johnson of the
> Rescue Steam Fire Company, in honor of being the only
> colored chief engineer in the state of Virginia. It will be
> presented by John Mitchell, Jr., editor of the Planet at
> Price's hall, (*Richmond Planet* 1899, 8 July)

The Progressive Club held a grand X-ray Bazaar for five consecutive
nights at Price's hall to benefit the Richmond Hospital Association. The
X-ray bazaar took place during April 1903, and the admission price was
15 cents. On May 25, 1903, the Negro Business League of Richmond met
at Price's hall to reorganize and prepare to attend the national session in
Nashville. The Municipal orchestra had a two-week engagement at Price's
hall during January 1917.   The Uniform Rank, Knights of Pythias
celebrated their anniversary on October 2, 1899 and sponsored the banquet
along with a street parade:

> By 11 o'clock, the spacious parlors and reception hall at Mr.
> A. D. Price's new establishment were filled with men attired
> in showy uniforms and ladies in the latest fashions. It was a
> gay assemblage. Behind a wall of choice plants and flowers,
> Prof. Scott's orchestra played.
>   It was 12:30 A. M., the hour having been previously
> appointed before the grand march was played and the
> movement towards the spacious dining hall was made.
>   The table presented a magnificent appearance,
> decorated as it was with Pythian colors and potted plants.
>   Covers were laid for 100 persons, but this was found
> to be totally inadequate, and even after provisions had been
> made for more at the side tables, others were compelled to
> wait.
>   . . .It was 8 o'clock before the farewell was said and
> the jubilant knights sought the peaceful solitude of their
> inviting coaches, oblivious of the absence of the chivalric
> shield.

> The entire affair was unquestionably one of the greatest
> successes ever noted in the history of Pythianism in this city.
> (*Richmond Planet* 1899, 7 October)

These gatherings and club meetings continued at the Price funeral home
until Mrs. Price's death in 1934, when A. D. Price Jr., who took over the
business from his father in 1921, ceased renting out rooms. By 1934,
fraternal societies were less popular, more African American-owned space
existed and, probably the rental business was no longer profitable.

The community depended economically on A. D. Price Sr. for
transportation and funeral service, but they also benefitted from his
leadership in Richmond society. As a member of the "committee of
arrangements" with W.I. Johnson [another prominent African American
funeral director], A. D. Price organized the first grand excursion from
Richmond to Seaside Park. They made the following announcement about
Seaside Park:

> The only piece of water front that can be bought by Colored
> People on the broad Atlantic Ocean, most beautiful spot on
> the Virginia coast. Only 18 miles from Norfolk. Delightful
> summer homes for the colored people. (*Richmond Planet*
> 1899, 8 July)

This event in 1899 featured surf bathing, seafood, baseball games, concerts
and eloquent addresses by renowned orators. Another example of his
leadership in society was Price's role in the Richmond Neighborhood
Association fund-raiser in May 1920:

> The City Auditorium was the scene of one of the most
> beautiful pageants ever presented in this city, known as "the
> Million Dollar Wedding."
> Richmond appreciated the efforts of the management
> and responded with the largest audience ever assembled in
> that spacious edifice. Packed from pit to dome with standing
> room at a premium, the enthusiastic audience greeted each
> bridal party with round after round of applause.
> More than 600 participants! More than twenty bridal
> parties, each [vying] with the other in beauty and
> magnificence . . ..

Mrs. Ora Brown Stokes as bride and Mr. A. D. Price
as groom led the bridal parties in (*Richmond Planet* 1920,
15 May).

Mrs. Ora B. Stokes was president of the Richmond Neighborhood
Association and chose A. D. Price from all the available community
leaders to be her escort.

In business circles, A. D. Price earned respect for his management
expertise and successful business skills. Stockholders elected Price
president of the Southern Aid Insurance Company in 1905 and president
of the Evergreen Cemetery in 1917. During the early twentieth century,
many companies appointed Price to their board of directors, including the
Mechanics' Savings Bank, Capitol Shoe and Supply Company, Richmond
Hospital, and the American Beneficial Insurance Company. During A. D.
Price's business career, his funeral home profession allowed him to use his
cultural services and business skills to become an influential community
power broker.

Unfortunately, the same stubbornness and independent drive that
enabled him to be a successful entrepreneur also was the cause of his
death. Finding a callous growth on the bottom of his left foot, Price
decided to become his own surgeon and operated on himself. This
personal operation on March 26, 1921 left him on crutches. An infection
set in, and on April 7, he entered the Richmond Hospital where a team of
surgeons amputated his left foot above the ankle to save his life. Although
in good spirits after the operation, he lapsed into a coma the following day,
and on the next day Saturday, April 9, A. D. Price died. He left a
personal estate worth $53,102 upon his death (*Richmond Planet* 1921, 21
May).

A. D. Price's prominent position in the community is largely
attributable to the respect of his business skills and the reverence bestowed
on his profession. The community granted W. I. Johnson, Price's arch
rival and former partner, similar stature. Johnson and Price were partners
for approximately fifteen months between 1893 and 1898. The end of their
partnership left bitter feelings that lasted the rest of their lives (*Richmond
Planet* 1919, 29 November). When Price began building on 210 and 220
East Leigh street, Johnson matched him by putting up a structure around
the corner on 207 Foushee street. In April 1911, W. I. Johnson sold his
property at 207 Foushee street for $25,000 to the white Eagle family.
Simultaneously, Johnson purchased three houses at 10, 12, and 14 W.

Leigh street with a total front footage of sixty feet. He tore these houses down to construct a spacious three-story building for his enterprises.

While the Price complex was a set of separate buildings with specialized functions, Johnson chose to build a single, immense building. The brick, three-story structure is still commercially used today. The front of the building on Leigh street is three bays. However, after going back forty to fifty feet toward the rear, the entire building expands two additional bays to the left. On the front of the building is a stone placement with the inscription "1911." While A. D. Price chose to have separate meeting rooms on the top two floors over his funeral home, Johnson built his second floor as a wide-open space without interior partitions. This large open space allowed Johnson to hold many different types of civic activities, including Virginia Union University basketball games. When the African American community decided to stage major basketball games in Richmond, they went to funeral director W. I. Johnson for space:

> *Big Teams on Way Here*
> *Negro Welfare League Constructs*
> *Basket Ball Courts*

> The mid-winter sport of basketball has invaded the South and there is no longer any necessity of a long trip to New York to see an interesting contest, for arrangements are under way to bring all the big school teams to Richmond.
> The court and outfit will be furnished by the Richmond Welfare League, which has recently fitted up Johnson's Auditorium for the Public School children's use. The games will be furnished by the Athletic Association of Va. Union—Union on one hand, Virginia Union—with Hampton, Howard, Lincoln and Petersburg as her prospective opponents (*Richmond Planet* 1916, 8 January).

Both Price and Johnson cultivated social roles within the Richmond community beyond simply providing funeral services. Their rivalry for business and social status took place within four blocks of each other. It is unimportant why one chose to construct a building to support basketball, while another housed secret society meetings. Both men envisioned their professional positions in the community to include extensive civic responsibilities, as displayed in the artifacts and buildings they constructed and left behind.

However, using newspapers and interviews to develop the characteristics and beliefs of A. D. Price is problematic. This method requires the author to decipher each source's perspective and derive an "objective" perception of A. D. Price from potentially bias sources. The next section on R. C. Scott erases this uncertainty. Because the next section is R. C. Scott's autobiography, it as an accurate view of how one funeral director perceived his role in society. The author builds the rest of the study around this view.

R. C. SCOTT

Foreword

On June 23, 1953, Robert C. Scott, Sr., began furnishing the facts which are contained in this treatment of his life.

At intervals from that time until shortly before his death on November 1, 1957, he would make available information which is herein contained.

This may be considered an autobiography in the sense that, the vast majority of this material was dictated and supervised by him. Or, you may want to feel that it falls short of an autobiography because it was not completed by him. Had his health permitted, he would have.

At any rate, that very small portion which deals with, roughly, the last several months of his life, has been added for the one purpose of completing it.

A conscientious effort was made to check-out for accuracy, all of that posthumous portion with the view in mind that this could be considered authentic, representative biography, if not an autobiography.

I offer no apology for the amateurish literary results. I do however, attest that truth was a much higher priority than literary style for which I was shooting.

There never has been an assignment that I have taken deeper interest or pride in. I further hope that, the part that was mine to do, puts that part that was done by him, in such focus as may inspire. This was his stated desire and intention in the first place.

Anthony J. Binga

I, Robert Crafton Scott, was the first child of Alpheus Scott and Angie Wilson Scott. I was born in Richmond, Virginia, on the first day of May 1888 in a house that is at this time, 1108 North Thirtieth Street. My only sister, Cleopatra, was born in Richmond, Virginia in 1890.

I remember my mother very well although I was only eleven years old when she died. I remembered her burial in the lower part of Oakwood Cemetery. I remembered her as a very small, lightly complexed person with the most beautiful long black hair which fell down her back way below her waist. I always understood that her parents were of Indian descent. Many times during her life time and after her death, she was referred to as having been a beautiful woman, although my father said she never weighed more than ninety pounds. She was a very stern and positive person, tho warm and loving.

My paternal grandparents are most vivid in my recollection. They lived a distance out from Richmond that seemed to me then to be at least ten to twelve miles. Really, it was not that far. In fact it is almost within the limits of present Richmond.

To be exact, the tract of land which belonged to my grandfather was a part of the site which is now Richard Byrd Airport. A portion of this area during World War II served as one of the largest training fields for Army aviators. During the war it was called the Richmond Army Air Base.

Many days my mother sent Cleo (the affectionate name we called my sister) and me down to my grandfather's house. I always enjoyed these excursions because I would have an opportunity to see the cattle, horses and chickens and some other sights that city children missed. Most of our trips, if not all, to our grandparents' were made on foot. This is likely why it seemed such a long distance to us.

It was a rare treat to ride back with grandfather in his wagon being pulled by his horse "John." What a thrill it was to be allowed to drive "John." When my grandfather came into town, he usually brought vegetables, eggs and butter and the like to sell at the market. I recall on numerous trips to grandmother's I would take a bucket with me to bring it back full of clean, fine, white sand which was plentiful around grandmother's place. You might imagine how long it might have taken for a ten-year-old boy to walk several miles with a bucket full of sand, stopping on the way to play and rest. Our mother taught us to use this sand to scour our floors at home. The sand served the same purpose that abrasive detergents, which are abundant on the market today, serve. When one had finished scrubbing a wooden floor with this sand and it had been thoroughly done, it was the most beautiful white you can imagine. And I was the most tired ten year old in the neighborhood.

I think I can truthfully and accurately state that my life extended thru the most rapidly developing era in human history from the standpoint of inventions, customs changes, economic, social and racial progress, certainly in modern history.

In and about 1898, when I was ten years old, two things were going on so far as I was concerned. First, I was becoming old enough for things around me to influence me. This was just prior to the "turn of the century," just about the time that so very many things are dated from. I can recall the popular use of the telephone, the advent of the airplane, graphaphone, motorcycles, automobile, submarine tunnels, to say nothing of the purely electronic inventions such as the radio, electric street cars, escalators, sound movies and television. All of these things have come to pass during my life time. It has never ceased to be and probably never will, cease to be, to me, an interesting past-time to observe the changes that have taken place and the influences of these changes on people. This study, I feel, is greatly responsible for any success I may have attained. I was sure of one thing even then, I was not to be surprised at any change. The next thing was, I was to gracefully become a part of these changes and contribute to making them whenever possible if I expected to occupy any signal place in this world. I will come back to this later in an account of a relationship with my father.

Of the wars our country has been involved in during my lifetime, I was too young for action in the Spanish-American War of 1898. Because of a deferment based on a dependent, my first child, Grayce, who I will refer to later, I was not called to serve in World War I, 1918. The other two conflicts, World War II and the Korean conflict, I had exceeded enlistment age.

In my boyhood, I recall incidents connected with the Spanish-American War. During these times, newspapers were the only medium by which the news of the world was spread. Methods of communication and transportation were so slow that news of the close of the Spanish-American

War was at least a week getting to some parts of the country. As I recall my first self operated business venture was selling the special or extra editions of the *Leader* and *Dispatch* which carried accounts of the ceasing of hostilities. We kids used to buy them from the newspaper publishers at two for a penny and sell the "extras" as they were called, for one, two and three cents. Now, I'd say that the newspaper "house," as it was called, was fully four miles from my home. Needless to say, I walked, both ways.

I guess it must have been about 1895 when I started school which was then called the Henrico County School, a two room affair complete with pot-bellied stove and out-side "facilities." I remember vividly, always being anxious to learn. One of my teachers, I recall, was Mrs. Maggie Murray Epps. I also remember some of my teachers not having been kind to me. No doubt, one incident in my life at school had much to do with whetting my determination to follow my chosen profession.

The teacher asked the class once to recite on what they would like to become when they grew up. I promptly said that I wanted to be an "undertaker." Right before the class, this teacher laughed scornfully. This cut me deeply. That one experience at such an early age along with other hardships and handicaps, I am sure, inspired me to do the thing I most wanted to do.

In 1897, I was eleven years old and my sister Cleo was nine. Our mother was stricken with her last illness. After it became evident to her that she would not live long enough to rear us, she asked my father to send Cleo to live with a relative in the North, in the event she died. Upon my mother's death in 1897, my father kept his promise to my mother and sent Cleo North. This did not work out for Cleo's happiness. Although my father was a devout Baptist and a deacon in his church, as I will relate later, in spite of heavy criticisms he entered her in St. Emma's Catholic School in Powhatan County, Virginia, a boarding school of enviable reputation. I recall him as being a very warm man and endowed with an amazing understanding of his abilities as well as his limitations. I remember him having said that, he might be criticized for working his problem out in the way in which he did, but none of the critics had a better solution nor would they share any of the responsibility. He said he had a solution and he executed it. She was reared in a way that neither she or my father regretted. I heard him say more than once, it would have been his wish that he could have kept his family together, but without a mother and rather than run the risk of someone being unkind to us, he adopted this plan. I lived with him.

I had every reason to consider my father, Alpheus Scott, a God fearing Christian gentleman. He was a straight and stately man, often referred to as being handsome. I do not ever remember having heard him utter an oath of any kind. He was an ardent churchman and an active member of the Fourth Baptist Church, the church in which I hold membership. He served on its Trustee and Deacon Boards.

Before my mother passed, I recall two incidents. One of them involved him, my mother and me. The lessons I learned from these experiences have stuck with me thru the years. I pause to recite them because I know they enrichened my life and for whatever a recitation of them might afford one reading this, I would like for them to benefit also. The first incident occurred when my father was operating a shoe shop on North Ninth Street in the five hundred block. One of the chores I had to perform was to take my father's lunch to him which my mother had prepared; I can remember the little split wicker basket with the clean white napkin covering the food. I would have to carry it from my house on thirty first Street to his shop on Ninth Street, a distance of about three miles, as one walked. When I got to his shop, I saw him talking to a very attractive lady. As soon as I returned home, I told my mother of what I had seen. She evidently remonstrated with him about what I had observed and recited. He did not say anything to me when he returned. But the next time I brought his lunch to the shop he told me, "Son, never kill the goose that laid the golden egg." He had a way of telling you something in a way that it stuck with you, perhaps more vividly than had he stirred up a fuss. That was just his way. Since then, however, I have tried awfully hard to attend to my own business and leave other people's alone, particularly if I did not understand. The incident was innocent enough, I am sure. However, I had put a different meaning on it simply by tattling.

The other experience involved my father and me and this also taught me an invaluable lesson. I give equal importance to this that I give to the unhappy experience I had in school with the teacher who challenged my ambition. I am sure my father saw a lot in me when I was a youngster which he wished to develop. I was not unlike most youngsters, in that, I was attracted by some of the things of life that, to a boy glittered. However, my father, in his stern, warm and firm way, always tried to help me to put things in proper focus.

Right around the "turn of the century," I began selecting friends, as boys do. Some of the boys I began going around with were much older than I. They smoked, cursed, swore, drank and wore the most stylish clothes which all adds up to girls and women. Of course, in order to lead this kind of life in 1903 a youngster had to work all day, every day. This meant quitting school. My father wanted more than anything for me to go to school and prepare myself for better things than those calculated to be attained the way I was going then. He was not forceful often. By and large he was friendly, peaceful and amiable, very slow to anger and deeply in love with Cleo and me.

This particular day, I remember clearly, he called me aside and told me this, "Robert, I want you to go to school. I want you to take every advantage of every opportunity in which you may be able to learn. You now want to hang with the gang working in the tobacco factory. This is as far as they will ever get. I can not make you go to school nor can I make you learn at school. But I can and am going to see that you learn my trade." Incidentally, you may recall my having mentioned taking his lunch to him at his shoe shop. He was a first class shoemaker. In those days lots of the shoes, in fact most, were made by artisans. Factory made shoes were a rarity. He taught me to build a shoe right from a pattern. In those days, people placed orders for one or more pairs of shoes after having selected the leather and style much as one does in selecting material and pattern from yard goods in a tailor shop for a suit of clothes. The shoemaker kept the patterns of his customers and was able to fill orders in this manner. This was quite a trade at that time. He saw to it that I learned his trade at his shoe last and bench. Many times have I thanked him for not letting me work in the tobacco factory. I hasten to say, he was altogether right. I number among my friends today, broken men who were these boys, some of them on meager pensions from a job that took most of their lives and gave very little in return in the way of comforts and security.

About 1905 my father became interested in, what was then known as, the "Undertaking business." I do not recall that he ever exactly said so, however, I have often felt that he abandoned his shoemakers' trade for the business and profession of Funeral Directing, largely for my benefit, to inspire me and give me the opportunity I said I wanted.

Being an aggressive person, by nature, I seriously think that my ambition was more than my father understood. I can recall the numbers of times I had ideas and plans of improving his business. He being an older man and not given with quite as much aggressiveness was not inclined to see business operations and methods in the same light as I. In 1906 I was licensed as an embalmer by the Virginia State Board of Embalmers holding license number five. I was eighteen then and likely the youngest licensed embalmer, certainly one of the youngest.

Right at this time in the history of Funeral Directing and Embalming in the State of Virginia and city of Richmond was a very important period. It may be remembered that the Civil War of the 1860's had given embalming, in its modern application, it's greatest impetus. History has it that so many of the soldiers from the North who were killed here in the South were shipped back home for internment. In order to facilitate this practice, embalming met a great need. After the war, the practice became more widespread. Of course this was consistent with the resulting health protection requirements growing out of urbanization. All of this was going on about the same time. Although, at the time I passed the Board to practice embalming which was some forty years after the war, the freezing method of preserving was still practiced to a large extent. This involved the use of a cooler into which the remains of a human, after death, were placed and large chunks of ice were placed around it. There was a drip pipe in the bottom of the cooler and a pan to receive the melting ice. Just before the time scheduled for the funeral services, the remains were dressed and viewed by the family and friends.

One's imagination would not have to be very vivid to appreciate how unreliable, unsanitary and generally unpleasant this whole procedure was. However, with all of these phases of the profession to endure, I always felt that there was a better way. I was always on the lookout for better ways others had discovered and I found a few and better ways myself.

During the time I was working for my father, I availed myself of every opportunity to educate myself by reading everything I could get my hands on relating to the very latest methods and techniques known at that time. I also lost no opportunity to educate the people in the community to the virtues of embalming. There were other modern ideas I would have interjected into my father's business had he allowed me to. It has turned out that I was right. But at that time there was no way of telling than by taking the calculated chance. This he was not inclined to do, leaning toward conservatism. Needless to say, there were other firms in the city and state who were adapting a progressive approach. Some of these firms frequently called upon me for my professional services which assisted me in building and broadening my reputation.

I remember once suggesting to him to allow me to enter into partnership with him in his business. I recall, he took me out to the front of his place which was then located in the Thirty hundred block on "P"

Street, pointing to the sign which was painted across the front of the building, he said, "Robert, you see my name painted up on that sign, Alpheus Scott, it will stay there until it rots down or burns down." He said this in a kindly but positive way. With competition in the field sharpening and opportunity broadening, it required the type of approach, I later found out to be correct, the one which I had in my mind.

Our people generally did not have very much resource to do for them the things they wanted done, which is often the case. They wanted embalming and appreciated the tasteful funeral service for their loved ones. They knew it was a symbol of sociological progress. It was up to the progressive practitioner to provide these things consistent with their ability to pay for them.

Things during this time were very rough with my father too. I remember on one occasion a white bill collector came to call on him. There were many of them then. I hasten to say, he never ran from or refused to see any of them, although he did not have the money with which to pay them, always. He would graciously invite them back, with the statement, usually, he hoped to have money when they returned. However, this particular bill collector talked to my father in a way that made me determine in my mind that I would operate my affairs in such a way that a man would have no reason to talk to me like he talked to my father.

It was sometime during the first of 1910. I approached my father to tell him that I decided to go into partnership with a man by the name of John Lewis. The firm was operated finally as Lewis and Scott, Undertakers and Liverymen. Lewis was already in the seafood business. He had a few friends but did not have the interest or inclination in the funeral service profession I had. Some idea of this partnership may be gained from our agreement which I retain among my papers. I had little money, but I knew the business.

We operated our business from 2218 East Main Street. In connection with funeral directing and embalming, as was the case of business of this period, we operated a livery concern, renting hacks as they were popularly called, for weddings and other social events. A fellow might decide he would hire a carriage for Sunday to carry him and his lady friend out for a drive. Among the horses we owned, one is vivid in my memory as outstanding because of his temperament which caused me to become very attached to him. His name was "Buster." He was my service buggy horse. Among my papers I have several pictures in which Buster appears.

The month of May, my birth month, marks the launching of my first business venture in 1910 with my partner. Nineteen-ten also marks the year I married the mother of my daughter, Grayce, Janie Epps. This union dissolved in 1944.

In the meantime, I was more determined than ever to be a first class Funeral Director for some of the same reasons every young man with an up and coming family has, for wanting to succeed. Grayce, my daughter, was born before I had been married 2 years.

My partnership with John Lewis lasted not quite two years. As I had fore-mentioned, Lewis was not particularly interested in the profession. So for reasons affecting the best interest of us both, I bought John Lewis' interest out.

It remains with me clearly that the practice of embalming was still relatively in its infancy and the public, to begin with, did not catch on to the advantages quickly. Their reason was primarily economic. Being economically handicapped, and just less than two generations out of slavery, did not make it easy to sell so revolutionary and expensive a practice. However, after I bought my partner out, I was free to do those things which I thought would materially improve the profession and subsequently myself.

I began by selling the public on the relative hygienic advantages of embalming which was a real threat in this new urban society which was rapidly developing. I felt that I wanted to advance the general health of our urban community to the extent that I provided facility in my establishment for the purpose of accomplishing the process more professionally than could possibly have been done in the home. In the absence of professional facilities in the funeral homes, embalming was being done in the residence particularly when death occurred there. My new facility broadened the usefulness of my funeral home.

One instance I recall vividly during this period was one in which a lady who had utter confidence in me but had misgivings about the "new fanged embalming" engaged me to serve her at the death of her daughter. The girl had died of some lingering illness. The mother questioned me minutely about the technique which I used, which, of course, was the latest accepted technique of the time. She had been lead to believe that a very desecrating method was generally used. I am reluctant to say that some embalmers did use a very revolting method. At any rate, I outlined my technique to the mother which seemed to have met with her approval. Years after, this mother admitted to me that while the girl's remains were resting in the house, she took all of her garments off to assure herself that what I promised her would be done, I had done. This gives some idea of how skeptical people were at that time.

I maintained my business at 2218 East Main Street until 1920 at which time I purchased 2223 East Main street, directly across the street. This is the building which houses our main office and main chapel, at present.

As I recall my first big real estate venture, I can not forget the famous John Mitchell, who at that time was President of the Mechanics Savings Bank of Richmond, a Negro institution. I clearly remember bringing him down from his office to look at the building I proposed to purchase. I outlined to him my ideas relating to the multiple purpose use the building could be made to serve with some renovations. In his famous "horse trading" manner, he said, "Scott, I'm going to open a credit account for you at my bank from which you may draw the money necessary to do what you want to do." As I reflect, Mitchell caught the enthusiasm of my desire to progress and bring our people some more of that which they so sorely needed. I think you will share the opinion that it demonstrated an unusual amount of faith and confidence in me and my ability. Needless to say, I justified this faith and confidence. Many times after I went into my new building, Mitchell would stop by and give words of encouragement and helpful suggestions.

Fraternal orders such as the St. Lukes, Good Samaritans, King David, Sons and Daughters of Rescue, Elks, Reindeer, Cup of Cold Water, Buzzards, National Ideal and many others, were quite popular in those days. They afforded an outlet for "belonging," aside from the financial benefits which were derived. Built into the fraternal aspect of the orders was usually a sick benefit and death benefit for their members.

When I moved into the new and larger three story brick building, I had ample space to renovate and remodel it to do most anything I wanted. Tying my profession to the community, I renovated the building in such a way as to provide ample facilities to accommodate the "secret orders," as they were called, and their meetings. During this time there was a meeting of some one or more of the organizations each night in the week including weekends. There were four of these "lodge rooms" on the second floor. This brought quite a number of people into my place constantly thru a central door to the funeral home. The social and economic life of the community revolved around the secret orders because for obvious reasons, the most influential people belonged and usually headed the various lodges. To extend my influence, became easy thru contacts made from these organizations. Whereupon I became a chronic joiner. I took a deep sense of pride in these opportunities to meet, know and help people. At a time during this period, I belonged to some twenty five or thirty organizations. Lots of them have gone out of existence now, however, I take great pride still in my membership in the Thebans, Oriental, Astorias Clubs. These are all clubs of men whom I have known for more than fifty years. In more recent years I was initiated into the Omega Psi Phi Fraternity and have joined the Old Timers Club.

To give some idea of the impact of this "secret order" regime, they used to "turn out," that is, be represented, usually in a body at the funeral of one of the members. There were ritualistic ceremonies, regalia, bands, wakes, feasts, etc. All of these were closely associated with the economic and social life of the community. I can recall vividly cases in which a member of the community belonged to as many as four or five of the orders. As a part of the final rites, there was included marching to the church and to the cemetery behind a ten to twenty-five-piece band playing marches and dirges, with the less active members forming an entourage of horse drawn hacks and carriages. The Christian ceremony, the written and verbal testimonies, the grave-side rituals, the time consumed marching to the church and to the cemetery, more frequently than not, required some four or five hours, depending upon how far removed the places were from each other.

I remember upon one occasion, one of the members of one of these lodges died in the midst of the meeting in the lodge room. A competitor, Caddie Price's hearse backed up to the front door of my funeral home and took the man's remains away. This classically points out the matter of individual choice which prevailed just as it should have.

During the winter of 1919 and into 1920 the country experienced an epidemic of influenza. This was one of the most devastating epidemics of modern time. I remember working right around the clock for days on end. By this time, embalming had taken quite a hold, but people were dying so rapidly that it was not humanly possible, because of the lack of licensed embalmers to properly embalm and sterilize all of the victims. It was an accepted fact that the lack of sterilization of the victims was responsible for the spread of the disease and its subsequent toll.

Not long after, the horse-drawn hearse and hack gave way to the automobile, limousine and motor hearse. During this transition it was very interesting and at times amusing sight to see a funeral cortege moving thru the streets composed of horse drawn hearse, hacks, carriages, automobiles, buggies and these bands I mentioned before. It was quite some while, however, before the motorized hearse enjoyed general public acceptance. You might imagine how difficult it might have been to maintain the dignity comparable with the occasion when a normally well-mannered and evenly-tempermented equine, so selected for his poise and bearing, would suddenly bolt to the astonishment of equally poised hearse or hack drivers and to the subsequent chagrin of the mourners at the backfiring of one of the automobiles whose disposition because of its design refused to be throttled down to seven or eight miles per hour to keep from either leaving the procession behind or to avoid running over that part in front. This attempt on the part of one other than x-horse drivers to restrain the contraption to a slow speed would frequently result in overheating the engines. It should not be difficult to imagine the consternation of persons and horses to see a great white cloud of steam coming down the street in the midst of all of the other pageantry and then suddenly an explosion from the balking automobile which is being made to run roughly one half as fast as the slowest speed it was designed for. The horse nearest the commotion let out a characteristically distressing wail which could be heard by the very last pair of horses at the end of the procession. Then it was on, surely enough. Those were the good old days.

Realizing this kind of situation could not endure and being conscious of the steady progress being made with the automobile, I felt that one of the greatest contributions I could make to the community and my business was to install all motor equipment. This transition was not easy for a lot of reasons, some of which I have mentioned, then too it was very expensive. However, I was determined to give my community what I felt it needed and deserved and in a short time I had completely motorized to become the first funeral director in our community to motorize one hundred per cent. That is, hearses, limousines and service cars.

I would not want to pass over this era completely without mentioning again, my first call service buggy horse, "Buster." He was one of the finest horses I ever owned and I have owned many. In my day, I have seen some "ornery critters" too. Some horses will not work with but one particular horse. I have seen some horses too proud to work in the sense that as long as there was a crowd watching, he would go thru all of the motions of pulling his share of the load. However, when a hill was reached, the other horse hitched up with him was obliged to do most of the pulling. This is an example of being lazy and vain. I remember other horses who never exerted too much energy unless they were under the stress of a whip. Horses have lots of sense. I know this from my own

experiences with them. I learned lots from them and learned to love them.
I found out that there is not too much difference between horses and men
in some respects.

In the middle twenties I was invited by Mrs. Maggie L. Walker,
who was at that time president of the St. Luke Penny Savings Bank, to
serve on the board of that bank. I served for several years. When I
discovered that my membership on the bank board was curtailing my
ability to borrow and expand my business because of a banking rule
relating to directors, I reluctantly resigned. Mrs. Walker was reluctant in
accepting my resignation. There remained mutual admiration between us
which is borne out in my many subsequent pleasant affiliations. Others on
the bank board at this time were men who prior to this period, during this
period , and later, were men whom I was thrown with intimately in various
other business endeavors. One of them I recall particularly was, J.
Thomas Hewin, a highly respected attorney. In fact, it was Mr. Hewin
who drew up the agreement relating to my partnership with John Lewis.
Thru the years he has served me as my attorney and has served as the
attorney for my firm. Mr. Hewin is my daughter, Grayce's great uncle.
He was chairman of the bank board during my tenure. Others, I might
mention, were, Spottswood W. Robinson, Jr., a boyhood pal; a real estate
broker and attorney, Dr. Leon A. Reid, Sr.; and Charles T. Russell, an
eminent architect. Professor Russell designed and contracted for the work
incidental to remodeling and renovations I made at my neighborhood
chapels, of which I will mention later.

Prior to 1930 there existed two other banks here. The Second Street
Bank of the Richmond Beneficial Insurance Company and the Commercial
Bank of the Southern Aid Insurance Company. In 1930 these two banks
merged with the St. Luke Penny Savings Bank to become the Consolidated
Bank and Trust Company. Later, I will mention more about a young man
whom I took an interest in, but as relates to the bank, I influenced him and
exerted influence to have him take a place on the Board of the Consolidated
Bank and Trust Company that I had occupied on the board of one of the
member banks. He became a member of the Board in 1951. This young
man's name is Anthony J. Binga.

I was steadily building my business all through the middle and later
1920's along lines I felt would make it sound as well as enduring. Up to
this time, numbers of other men had started like businesses and had failed
for various and diverse reasons. I was most interested in my own
business. But I took a keen objective interest in these businesses which

failed. In other words, those practices, policies and methods that the firms
which failed had used, I tried to avoid. One of my policies has been
"Charity yes, but charity tempered with prudence". I knew because it had
been proved that a firm could not continue to serve families and not get
paid for services rendered and stay in business. I knew that the only way
I would be able to continue to grow along with the rapidly growing
economy of these times was to get paid for whatever services and
merchandise I furnished.

The secret orders were still existing to a more limited extent. A
new economic device was attracting our people and logically so.
Insurance, that is, life insurance was beginning to more adequately meet
our economic needs. They were stronger and more able to provide more
dollars for less cents.

Some of our older insurance companies had been in operation for
some years but as the economic structure of the country changed, the
development of machines and manufacturing methods advanced, the city
attracted country people with higher wages and shorter hours. These
influences affected not only the economic life but the social life as well.
Since the fraternal orders met both a social as well as an economic need in
the community, any change would resultantly effect the fraternal movement
which it surely did. This change was not particularly sudden. But it was
steady and the orders fell into decline just as rapidly as this new economic-
social order was taking over.

I have discussed this widely because it had a direct influence on the
funeral service profession and on my own business in which I was
particularly interested. I thought of my interest in the fraternal orders as
being triple barreled. First it gave me an opportunity to help educate my
people along lines of what dignified funeral services were. This was an
educational program which my competitors had neglected. Next, it put me
in intimate contact with the "brothers and sisters" of my lodges and clubs
which placed me in a better position to educate them along lines toward
which I had been exposed in my business relations, to inspire them to
improve themselves and prepare themselves in appropriate ways to take
full advantage of the upsurge which was so very evident. This I must have
accomplished if I might judge from words and acts of thanks and
appreciation coming from some who said I helped and inspired them. And
last and equally important, it was from the funds or "death benefits" of the
fraternal organizations that up until this time, 99% of funeral expenses
were borne. I felt that if I received support from the fraternal orders, I
should make some contribution greater than just paying my "assessments,"

as the financial support was called.

As I adopted a policy of prudent charity, I adopted the policy that whoever it was that could or would not pay ten to twenty five cents a week for insurance protection, could or would not be able to pay $10.00 to $25.00 a month on a funeral of some member of the family. This may be a humorous way to reduce a policy to words, the fact was, I knew it made sense. To resolve my policy to more concrete terms, I made for myself a reputation of not selling anyone something that they were unable to buy and pay for.

Many of the ideas I executed, policies I adopted and programs I initiated in my business and made available to my clients, I secured from contacts I made thru affiliations with the National Associations of Funeral Directors, with individual members and the annual conventions which I rarely missed. I pleasantly recall Safell of Detroit, Tom Fraser of Washington, John Rhines of Washington, late C.V. Wilson of Lynchburg, late Roy Clarke of Roanoke, Mrs. Jennie Morris of Philadelphia, late James Wilkerson of Petersburg, Handy Beckett of Philadelphia, late Toland Edwards of Augusta, Ga., late Lawton Pratt of Jacksonville, Florida, and George Coleman of West Palm Beach, Fla. (father-in-law of my Olivia's brother, Reginald. I will again refer to Olivia more fully). These are all top flight progressive morticians. Some of the country's best. These names bring back pleasant memories spent in building our National Association. Some of them I nearly always found when I visited Hot Springs, Ark., which I did very frequently for months of rest. I recall it was at the National Association Convention in Philadelphia at which time I subscribed for my life membership in the National Association for the Advancement of Colored People along with a number of other funeral directors from all over the country. In my earlier and more active days I recall traveling with C.P. Hayes of Richmond, who was at the time National President, on extended trips, building the National Association. This time and money was a personal sacrifice made by all of us who believed that such an organization was necessary to improve the profession. Another person who, at one time, served as a dynamic National General Secretary, I remember warmly, Robert R. Reid. He did much to make the morticians of the country, association conscious.

I have spent lots of time and lots of money over the years on behalf of professional associations. I gathered much too. I may be accurate in saying that after visiting funeral homes all over this country, I was inspired to spend, in 1932 - 1934, nearly $50,000.00 to renovate my places. I do not say so to brag, it was true, our firm had a system of the most modernly appointed mortuaries in this country among Negroes, at that time. Professor Charles Russell supervised this entire project. I consistently affiliated myself with local, state and national professional associations. I am quite proud of a jeweled pin which was presented to me in 1957 as honorary past president of the Richmond Funeral Directors Association. Binga, my manager, happened to have been the president of the association that year and presented me with the pin at a special ceremony.

As the economic conditions of my people improved, they wanted better things with which to live better, a very natural and noble aspiration. They wanted and were providing for themselves and their children, better jobs, more education, better homes and other things consistent with these.

In the mid-twenties I met Anthony H. Turner, who was at that time business manager of St. Paul Industrial School at Lawrenceville, Va. Turner, at that time was married to the daughter of the President of the school, Arch Deacon Russell. This wife has since died. Sometime after her death he resigned from the position with the school and went into semi-retirement and has since devoted all of his time to securities and investments of various kinds. Thru his close friendship and tutelage, I have been able to take advantage of his wide knowledge and experience and astuteness in matters relating to securities. A. N. Turner is a highly respected and successful investor and counselor. He is a close and valued friend. His present wife, Ara and my present wife, Olivia, of whom I will speak later again, have developed a comparable friendship. Thru the Turners, I met the Right Reverend David W. Harris, Protestant Episcopal Bishop of Liberia. It was he who christened our son Bobbie of whom I will speak more about later. The Turners are Bobbie's godparents.

Shortly before 1925, the trend of our population was moving west, broadening out Old Jackson Ward. In 1925, sensing this trend, I purchased a parcel of property at 19 West Clay Street. The general idea behind this plan was that my people were becoming two and three family house dwellers. My place on Main Street served one definite purpose. But the people in the newly populated areas did not have the facilities at their homes to serve the purpose a neighborhood funeral chapel would serve. Hence, the initiation of my first Neighborhood Chapel.

Speaking of Jackson Ward, during this period of which I just referred, Adams Street which is just to the west of my place at 19 W. Clay Street, had added to it a thoroughfare, Chamberlayne Avenue beginning at Leigh Street, just one block away. It bisected Jackson Ward and handles quite a volume of traffic both vehicular and pedestrian.

On a visit back to his hometown once, my old friend Bill "Bojangles" Robinson, the famous tap dancer, was staying with me in my home as he did usually on his visits to Richmond. Riding thru that section on this occasion he noticed the volume of traffic at this wide intersection and remarked about the danger of it for the school children who had to cross the intersection on their way to Armstrong High School which is situated just to the west. He had me to stop the car as he observed the hazard. He vowed then that he would donate [to] the City of Richmond a traffic light which was absent at that corner. Whereupon a short time later, in July of 1933 at a ceremony attended by the Mayor, Dr. Fulmer Bright, the Chief of Police, Jordan William Schwartzchild, and old friend of Bill's and a childhood associate, Judge A. Taylor Pitt another old friend of his, Judge Julien M. Gunn, a friend and other dignitaries of the city, he presented to the city on behalf of the children of Armstrong High School, a traffic light to control traffic at that busy intersection. That light stands on that corner today with an inscription on it setting forth its donor.

In order to further translate my imagination into reality, after purchasing and remodeling my first neighborhood chapel, I purchased, in 1931 another parcel of property at 1401 Idlewood Avenue in anticipation of the exodus of our population further west. In the late 30's, there arose an obvious demand for neighborhood type facilities on Church Hill. Whenever the occasion arose, I would throw my home at 711 North 29th Street open at the disposal of my clients and friends in this section of our city. So, by this time, in addition to our main chapel at 2223 East Main Street, we were operating three Neighborhood Chapels, as they were called. My firm was the only firm which offered this type of service to the citizens of Richmond. These four places, all steam heated and strategically located, gave us a complete coverage of the Negro population at that time. All of the professional and business operations were carried on at only the main office. The other chapels were simple home-like parlor facilities for viewing and for funeral services, when either or both of these functions would more nearly meet the requirements of our families in these areas.

I might mention that, during the ten or twelve years since 1928, there had come into being some ten or more firms to be added to the seven or eight already operating at that time. This gives me mixed emotions as I appraise the profession. I recall with sincere regret that not all of the practitioners who came into the profession were dedicated to the high standards that, I along with several of the other firms, attempted to maintain.

The period immediately following the depression which actually dates, as you may recall from the stock market crash of October 1929, there occurred many changes and hardships. As a financial fact of life, I recall vividly that I did not, nor did mortuaries generally, feel the depression immediately as some other businesses which offered other services or even merchandise, did. I always felt that this was accountable to the very nature of insurance which had become the very financial life blood of funeral homes by this time.

Insurance had been carried over a long period of years which represented quite an investment. They were zealously held on to, with the determination that its protection would be the last or certainly among the very last assets a family would scuttle. Several years after the country's financial recovery, morticians started to actually feel the depression. It was during the period when the country was generally recovering, that the funeral director frequently came upon situations in which families had finally found it necessary to suspend their insurance programs out of dire need for premium money for subsistence.

Because of this chain of circumstances which I have just recited, I found that I was able to share with the less fortunate during this dark period. We secured lists from reliable sources like ministers, doctors and social workers and for three years, during the winter, I saw to it that grocery baskets containing substantial amounts of food were distributed among the families regardless whether they were clients or families we had served. I recall one of the years it was Christmas time. We needed five automobiles to distribute the baskets all over town. I can testify to one thing in connection with this, I have never before realized such a deep and abiding happiness as I did from the faces and lips of the adults and children of more than one hundred fifty families with whom I shared.

Human nature being what it is, insurance was not the first thing a family purchased after having been unemployed and after having to rely on soup lines for food and dole for clothing. Some of the other things which a family had found need to deprive themselves of got priority, then insurance protection. Then another two or three years was necessary for insurance of some types to have full benefit and value.

These comments came to mind to mention in order to bring into sharper focus the correlation between the funeral service profession and life insurance underwriting as it makes up the social-economic picture on the one hand and how insurance became a part of my life on the other.

During this period, in fact, until the mid 30's, there were adjustments of various and diverse kinds in nearly all businesses. The large financial institutions, particularly banks and insurance companies, found that, in order to weather the economic storm which had wiped out many fortunes and bankrupted thousands of businesses, it became necessary to merge or reorganize. One of the reorganization techniques was used in connection with the afore mentioned Consolidated Bank and Trust Company which occurred in 1930.

A technique of another sort was applied to the situation relating to one of our larger insurance companies, the National Benefit Life Insurance Company which was at that time operating in twenty six states.

In those days, insurance companies, like banks, did not have built into their structures some of the safeguards against failure in the presence of financial stress which they enjoy today. Many, in the wake of the '29 depression just folded up, went out of business and the policyholders were unable to recover any of their protection investment. The same fate was met by depositors in numerous banks. As we know, it is hardly probable that this kind of situation could occur again.

However, the company in point, being a mutual company, upon petition, finally endorsed by some 95% of the Virginia policyholders (stock holders, in a mutual insurance company) were able to retain sufficient assets of the company which had been forced into receivership as a result of the depression, enabling the Virginia policyholders of the National Benefit to reorganize and reestablish itself in Virginia.

Numbered among the Virginia policy holders who spearheaded a petition to Hon. Julien C. Gunn, Judge of the Circuit Court of the City of Richmond under whose jurisdiction the receivership fell, were Spottswood W. Robinson, Jr., B.T. Bradshaw, C. L. Townes, B. L. Jordan, W. A. Jordan, Dr. Leon A. Reid, H. A. M. Johns, C. D. Patience, A. J. Ruffin and others together with me.

I hasten to say that one of the greatest enjoyments and sources of pride of my life has been to watch the phenomenal growth and development of the Virginia Mutual Benefit Life Insurance Company, the name selected for the reorganized company, from the memorable date of January 24, 1933 when the Virginia State Corporation Commission granted the reorganized company its charter with Booker T. Bradshaw, President-Treasurer, C. L. Townes, Secretary-Manager, Vice Presidents, Dr. A. A. Tennant, H. A. M. Johns, Dr. Kyle Pettis, C. D. Patience and Dr. G. H. Francis. The capable and dedicated Booker Talmadge Bradshaw came to the Virginia Mutual bringing with him a rich experience and knowledge which he had gained as the Virginia supervisor of the original company.

I would not want to risk humility, but I believe I would be accurate if I stated that Judge Gunn's attitude and consideration relating to the future of the company as a Negro institution from [the] Board of Trustees level, was favorably tempered by his personal acquaintance with me growing out of a long and warm friendship between my dear friend, Bill "Bojangles" Robinson, and Judge Gunn. His consideration of S. W. Robinson, Jr., and me, I feel, was a prime factor that enabled the reorganized company to remain under Negro management with an integrated Board of Trustees. This view may be confirmed in light of the fact that the receivers which had been previously appointed to manage the company's affairs were all non-Negro until Judge Gunn's attention was drawn to it. Whereupon he appointed Robinson and me to serve along with the three original receivers. This group then became the Board of Trustees of the new company. These other three persons were Hon. Leon M. Bazile, Judge of the 15th Judicial District of Virginia; W. H. Cardwell, Attorney and Examiner of Records of the 10th Judicial District of Virginia and the late, John H. Dinnen, Jr., an attorney and insurance expert.

For a long number of years, Virginia Mutual was the only racially integrated insurance company of the Board and management level in our country.

My experience in race relations alone as they had to do with the operation of the company was wide and valuable and I hasten to say, an overall enjoyable one, over and above the enriching business and management experience it afforded me.

Second only to my pride in the intimate relations I have had with the Trustees and officers of Virginia Mutual is my service as chairman of the Finance Committee of the Board and after the death of S. W., Robinson, Jr., my chairmanship of the Board. Next, I cherish a warm relationship with Bill Cardwell and Judge Bazile. This was unique because of the character of the situation. Many times we have not agreed. But our relationships have been characterized [by] mutual and abiding respect for each other and his opinions.

In later years, men like David E. Longley, H. A. M. Johns and Richard W. Foster brought additional dignity, experience and stature to the Board. In my opinion Virginia Mutual is bound to grow and develop into one of the largest companies. It has the finest kind of foundation on which to build and it has the benefit of both young and seasoned men of unusual vision.

In 1936 I incorporated my business. I had several reasons for reaching the decision to do so. Prime among them was a desire to perpetuate what I had striven to build and I felt that a corporation was one of the surer ways. I was not altogether vain in wanting to perpetuate it. There were men who had been with me thru the years, Walter F. Preston, as an example, who had come with me in 1922, Anthony J. Binga, who came with me in 1931 and who married my daughter, Grayce in 1933. These men, I felt were capable of perpetuating the company in the event of my death. I became the corporation's president; Binga, its secretary-manager and Walter Preston, its treasurer. These offices have been held by this team since that time.

My grandchild, Rita Jane Mary Binga was born in March of 1935. She has ultimately worked with her mother in a florist business which I set up for and gave Grayce in 1948 after sending her to a floral designing school for training. Grayce operates under the name of "Rita Jane Florist" at 1401 Idlewood Avenue in a portion of this Neighborhood Chapel.

Concerning the perpetuation of the business, I might say that a simple recitation of my philosophy is that no man can dominate the stage of life forever. I look upon life as a stage upon which each man has an opportunity to give to the world his best, if he so chooses. After he has "done his dance," if he is a good actor, he will, in the best tradition of the stage, graciously bow to the applause and retire, thereby giving the other actors space to perform their part. Thru the years, I have attempted to train men in such a way that whether I exercise myself or not, the public and my clients particularly, had confidence in their ability because I demonstrated that I had. This sold them. I had sold myself, I felt they deserved an opportunity.

Over the nearly fifty years of my firm's existence, many persons have come with me and gone. Each made some contribution, each I tried to reward to the extent of my ability. During their employment some, like William Daniel, died in my employ, others had reasons of their own for feeling that they might better themselves by severing their relations with the firm. I feel that these persons too as well as myself have been enriched by our relationships.

Outstanding among the men who have worked with me is Walter F. Preston, whom I referred to before. He has worked with me longer than any other employee. Our firm gave him a testimonial celebrating his thirty-fifth year of service. He still serves as the company's treasurer. He and I have been thru some dark days together. These kinds of experiences have a way of cementing men together. I remember warmly, Moses Forsay, Thomas Smith, Walter J. Manning and many others.

On December 26, 1944, I married Miss Mattie Olivia Cumber who was teaching in the school system here. Beginning at our marriage, she has shared her time between being a homemaker and exercising interest in the firm, to the extent that during the earlier part of our marriage she served her required apprenticeship under me and in December, 1949, took the Board examination and was granted license to practice Funeral Directing. Beyond any shadow of a doubt she has been an outstanding asset to me and my business. She has made many contributions to my life, happiness and well being. I can not nor would I attempt to qualify the relative value of the many things she has done for me. I will say however, one of her most outstanding contributions was made on July 8, 1946 when she presented me with my only son, Robert C. Scott, Jr., who has added immeasurably to my life. I had mentioned both of them before. I will mention Bobbie again later.

In 1948 we purchased two Packard Hearses of the two, one was a Floral Funeral Coach. This piece of equipment represented the latest design in funeral coaches and it was the first car of its kind in the state. Beyond any doubt, it was outstanding and brought many favorable comments. It was designed in such a way as to provide for flowers on its top with provision for the casket inside. I recall my first airplane trip to Chicago along with Binga to drive this car back from the factory there.

As the years go by, now, naturally I have a deeper desire to perpetuate what has amounted to almost fifty years of hard work, for Bobbie.

I feel now that I have "done my dance" on the stage and I am quite willing to gracefully bow off and let the younger men and Bobbie have my space so that they may have the chance to receive the applause that I was favored with for so many years. I am retiring with the view in mind of extending my usefulness by counseling with persons who now have the strength and stamina I once had.

I am well aware that they will make mistakes just as I did. I realize I was not always right. I realize that they are going to try to dance their parts in terms of their abilities just as I tried. I do hope, however, I am leaving the stage a strong platform upon which they may be able to attract as appreciative audience as I was blessed with and that with all of the hardships the human race is plagued with, they can feel that their lives have been benefitted by having associated with me or having been a part of me as is the case of "Lit," "Bobbie," Grayce, Rita Jane, "Bing," and Preston.

[This ends the Autobiography of Robert Crafton Scott, Sr. as told to Anthony J. Binga, 1953-1957.]

SUMMARY

A. D. Price, W. I. Johnson, and R. C. Scott represent two generations of prominent Richmond funeral directors in the first half of the twentieth century. Price and Johnson were the pioneers of the profession. Unfortunately, their children were never able to maintain the earlier status of their fathers. When the "adopted son" of W. I. Johnson, George Johnson, took over the business upon W. I. Johnson's death in 1919, he died one year later himself. Other Johnson children attempted to run the business, but eventually the W. I. Johnson funeral home went out of business. When A. D. Price died in 1921, his son A. D. Price, Jr. did keep the business alive and it still exist today. However, the aggressive R.C. Scott successfully fought and outmaneuvered his less motivated rivals including the children of Price and Johnson. Scott demanded and secured a place in Richmond's business elite.

Despite their solicitous professional demeanor, these founders were contentious and assertive businesspeople. A. D. Price deliberately strove to outperform W. I. Johnson, and, because of his intense rivalry with Johnson, he built a business that surpassed most of the white funeral establishments in Richmond (*Richmond Planet* 1919, 29 November). R. C. Scott had a bad reputation for arriving before someone died and waiting for the potential client to become available (*Richmond Planet* 1916, 3 June). R. C. Scott also sued other embalmers because their state licenses were not in order (*Richmond Planet* 1929, 5 October). All three of these men were shrewd and pragmatic entrepreneurs.

R. C. Scott enjoyed an advantage in the competition because he used technology to differentiate his firm. The decision to motorize his complete funeral procession was bold, expensive, and technically necessary, but it was also a power statement. It raised the ante for elite status. He forced other prominent Richmond African American funeral directors to spend the necessary money to convert or accept second-class status. Because of his power play against the other African American Richmond funeral directors, Scott also far surpassed most white funeral directors. The power play was both public and professional. In a time when most whites did not own cars, R. C. Scott could boast he owned a fleet. He displayed this fleet daily in large processions (*Richmond Planet* 1927, 8 January).

Because of the intense competition among African American funeral directors, the successful competitors garnered respect and power from the community. These rivalries within the African American community exposed the entire Richmond community to constant innovations and aggressive marketing tactics. In this industry of unconstrained African American entrepreneurship, white firms followed the lead of their more progressive African American peers.

II
The History of Funeral Directing in America

INTRODUCTION

Caring for the dead is an essential and necessary function of human societies. Yet, it may be unrealistic to assume funeral rituals satisfy a basic, unchanging human need. Burial customs express a society's culturally-grounded ideas about death. Thus, a history of American funeral practices parallels and is a reflection of the historical and cultural transformations in the United States.

EARLY AMERICAN BURIALS

Before the middle of the nineteenth century, undertaking services were very rudimentary. An assortment of family members, neighbors, tradespeople, and the church worked together to complete the necessary undertaking tasks. The family first called a midwife to appear at the home and prepare the body for burial. Next, the family commissioned a local carpenter to build the coffin. If the burial took place at the church cemetery, the family then arranged with the church sexton to dig the grave. Between laying out the body and the actual burial, the family usually held a wake or watching. During this time, the family "watched" over the deceased and greeted visiting neighbors around the clock. Nearly all social and religious ceremonies used this general framework.

During the first half of the nineteenth century, certain tradespeople (sexton, cabinetmaker, liveryperson, etc.) began specializing in undertaking services. Eventually individuals combined these isolated auxiliary businesses and created a separate undertaking trade (Habenstein and Lamers 1955, 231). A. D. Price made this decision in 1886 and expanded his blacksmith and wheelwright business into the undertaking and livery business.

People entering the vocation initially found it difficult to engage in the trade full time. A lack of ready-made funeral paraphernalia made the trade time consuming and unprofitable. However, the arrival of coffin shops and coffin warehouses profoundly changed this barrier (Habenstein and Lamers 1955, 258). Due to the rapidly developing industrial base, manufacturers now found it economically feasible to mass produce coffins and create coffin warehouses around the country. These coffin warehouses put the most important component of the funeral at the undertaker's immediate disposal. Location was no longer a barrier to aspiring undertakers. An undertaker could telegraph an order to the closest warehouse and quickly replenish the company's limited stock.

COFFIN AND CASKET DEVELOPMENT

Since the coffin was the major variable in most funerals, it became a focal point and an instrument for social classification. Social customs usually dictated the other components in a funeral (the church, the cemetery, place of the wake, etc.). The family of the deceased set the tone and status of the funeral by the style, types of material, and fixtures chosen for the coffin. The full-time undertakers and their large selection of manufactured coffins from the coffin warehouses gave the survivors choices that the local cabinetmaker could not match.

This revolution in manufacturing techniques created a wide selection of coffins. Inventors filed patent applications for coffins out of iron, cement, marble, potter's clay, cement and wood, iron and wood, iron and glass, vulcanized rubber, aluminum, cloth and wood, and papier-mache during the nineteenth century. However, it was the Fisk Metallic Coffin that opened the door for mass production and mass distribution in the coffin-making industry. Almond D. Fisk received a patent for his invention in 1848. By 1853, Crane, Breed & Co. achieved mass production of this coffin and dramatically changed the industry. The top of the Fisk coffin was human-shaped with the arms folded (Illustration 3). The manufacturer claimed the form fitting style reduced the casket's weight and the amount of air locked in the casket. A coffin with less air prevented decay, according to Almond D. Fisk, because less air exhausted itself more completely (Habenstein and Lamers 1955, 264). Another major feature of the Fisk coffin was the glass plate over the head. This allowed the family to view the deceased without opening the coffin. Metallic coffins were also popular during this period because they provided greater protection during reburials. Relocating graves was common because of floods, vandals or urban expansion.

Between 1858 and 1862, designers introduced the modern rectangular style coffin. The introduction heralded a changed focus from simply containing the deceased to presenting the deceased aesthetically.

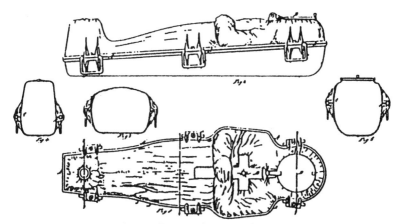

Fisk Metallic Burial Case, 1848, Patent Sketch

Illustration 3
Robert W. Habenstein & William M. Lamers. *The History of American Funeral Directing.* Milwaukee: Bulfin Printer, 1955; reprint, 1956. 263.

The industry also adopted the more progressive term 'casket' instead of 'coffin' as the common name for burial receptacles.

EMBALMING PROCEDURES

Only after undertaking developed into a trade was body preservation practiced in America. While various businesses engaged in undertaking part-time and the funeral was for the family and immediate community, there was no need to preserve the corpse. However, society's new focus on social status and aesthetic concerns in funeral presentations forced undertakers to explore novel ways to gain additional preparation time. In 1846, the patent office granted a patent to two undertakers for a "refrigerator for corpses." Their invention consisted of a common cooling board to hold the body, a concave ice-filled metal box that fit the torso, a lid, spigot, and handles (Illustration 4). The inventors discovered that freezing only the torso and chest adequately preserved a body. Since most funerals still took place in the home, the undertaker's ability to preserve people at remote locations was crucial. The self-contained cooling device allowed the deceased to stay clothed and preserved without lacerating the body. The invention became standard equipment for undertakers and dominated the market for twenty years because it was both portable and economical.

Cooling devices were impractical during the Civil War, and the family's insistence that deceased relatives return home for burial compelled the public to embrace chemical embalming (Habenstein and Lamers 1955, 336). While chemical embalming existed in Europe, it was not a commonly accepted practice there. In the U.S., society used the procedure sparingly before the Civil War. The public resisted chemical embalming because it felt the process mutilated the body and went against Christian doctrine. Only the medical profession administered the procedure before the Civil War. It was an expensive procedure and produced little profit for the undertaker.

The vast numbers of clients during the Civil War and the lack of any suitable alternative caused many surgeons, druggists, and chemists to become active military embalmers. After the war, most of these professionals abandoned the practice and returned to their previous occupations. Only the undertaker showed a willingness to conduct the procedure after the war. While entrepreneurial-minded undertakers viewed the procedure as a service for their clients, they lacked the technical skills to conduct the operation. Between 1855 and 1890, several chemical

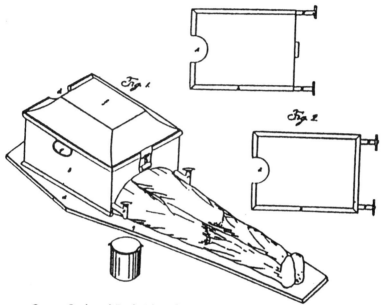

Corpse Cooler of Frederick and Trump, 1846. Top, an Actual Cooler,
Bottom, Patent Sketch

Illustration 4
Robert W. Habenstein & William M. Lamers. *The History of American
Funeral Directing.* Milwaukee: Bulfin Printer, 1955; reprint, 1956. 319

companies began manufacturing embalming fluids. These aggressive chemical companies sold their products through traveling sales agents. The sales agents promoted embalming to the undertakers and pressed them to adopt the procedure as a standard service. The companies even set up embalming schools to teach the technique and transform undertakers into competent technicians. Before 1900, most schools teaching embalming were commercial operations sponsored by chemical companies.

When R. C. Scott became a licensed embalmer in 1906, the freezing method of preservation was still prevalent in the Richmond African American community. R. C. Scott described the method as "unreliable, unsanitary, and generally unpleasant" in his progressive opinion. While the slow adoption of embalming techniques in Richmond's African American community was primarily economic, Scott built his business on revolutionary and innovative practices such as embalming. Scott's aggressive introduction of new practices stimulated the industry's rapid development in Richmond.

THE FUNERAL DIRECTOR PROFESSION

The emerging undertaker trade in the late nineteenth century slowly introduced liberal funeral reform. These reforms refocused the attention in funeral rites from the deceased, and transferred the attention to the well being and needs of the survivors. A 1913 *Outlook* article commented on the liberal funeral reforms:

> We have done much to Christianize our farewells to those who have gone before us into the next stages of life. We no longer darken the rooms that now more than ever need the light and warmth of the sun; we no longer close the windows as if to shut out Nature at the moment when we are about to give back to Mother Earth all that was mortal in the earthly career now finished; we no longer shroud the house in black, we make it sweet with flowers; for the hymns of grief we are fast substituting the hymns of victory; for words charged with a sense of loss we listen to words that hold wide the door of hope and vanished from our sight we no longer carve the skull and crossbones, the hourglass and the scythe- we recall some trait or quality or achievement that survives the body and commemorates the spirit. (Abbott 1913, 979)

Undertakers engineered the funeral's escape from solemnity and gloom to the Christian farewell described above. They achieved this by slowly taking control of the funeral and establishing conventions in their own fashion.

Urbanization threatened many traditional funeral customs. By the end of the nineteenth century, most urban homes were no longer large enough to hold the mourners, and transporting the body through narrow entrances and stairs was awkward. While more people in the late nineteenth century accepted the idea of embalming, executing the procedure in a crowded household was disquieting, even if partitions hid the procedure from view. Undertakers also found it distasteful to embalm in the home and transport their equipment from house to house. These problems eventually turned into opportunities for the undertaker.

Undertakers understood that to control their trade, they needed to bring each dimension of the funeral ritual under their influence. They gained control by combining permanent embalming labs, small dignified rooms for wakes, and chapels for religious and ceremonial services into single establishments. These operations were the forerunners of the modern funeral home. Once undertakers began to manage nearly all aspects of the funeral process, they adopted the title of funeral director and sought professional status. The funeral directors routinized the body preparation, supply of funeral paraphernalia, use of ceremonial facilities, and general funeral administration. This administrative act increased the time and opportunities for the funeral directors to give survivors professional services. The trade of selling commodities transformed into a profession of providing services.

R. C. Scott expanded on this model by seeking geographic control and profession control. In an attempt to capture the growing African American community, he created neighborhood chapels. His four strategically placed neighborhood chapels gave Scott access to the entire Richmond African American population. A client could use the up-to-date services of R. C. Scott and have the viewing or funeral service in their own neighborhood.

The undertakers became active in the association movement when they became occupationally self-conscious. While many local and state associations existed between 1865 and 1880, the first national convention of undertakers did not meet until June 22, 1882 in Rochester, New York (Habenstein and Lamers 1955, 463). Undertakers used the national association as a parent organization for state associations. They articulated two reasons for a national organization. First, they needed to develop guidelines to curtail unfair but legal competition within their ranks. Second, they wanted to bring a level of professionalism to the trade. In one of their first actions, they employed 'funeral director' instead of 'undertaker' in the association's name: National Funeral Director Association.

Using the public's escalating awareness of sanitation and germ theory, funeral directors lobbied their states to standardize and regulate embalming procedures.   In 1888, after negotiating with the National Association of General Baggage Agents, the two organizations adopted recommendations for transporting bodies by train. Most of the state health boards and the National Board of Health issued regulations based on these recommendations. The main component of the rules prohibited shipping a body unless a funeral director embalmed and disinfected the body. Thus, the funeral directors' embalming techniques secured professional recognition from the government. Only a funeral director had the authority to certify that a body was acceptable for shipment. In March 1894, because of the Virginia funeral directors' lobbying efforts, Virginia became the first state to ratify a regulatory embalming bill.

African Americans could not join the National Funeral Directors Association.

> The need for a separate association for Negroes, the white associations maintain, lies in the fact that while Negroes would be welcome, white representatives do not propose them as members, and hotels at which conventions are held will not give them room accommodations. It is also said that Negro undertakers face certain problems different from those of the white firms, such as the need to keep prices down in order to have greater assurance that the bills will be paid. (Bowman 1959, 98)

In 1925, African American funeral directors organized a separate national organization, the Independent National Negro Funeral Directors Association.   It later changed to The Progressive Funeral Directors Association and, in 1938, finally adopted the title National Negro Funeral Directors Association.   Contrary to the National Funeral Directors's rhetoric, the National Negro Funeral Directors Association had very similar goals and experienced little difficulty receiving payment.

Richmond African American funeral directors were very active in association activities on the national, state, and local level. C. P. Hayes from Richmond served as a president of the national association from 1939 to 1941 (Habenstein & Lamers 1955, 610) and R. C. Scott organized the first Virginia association meeting in April 1929 (*Richmond Planet* 1929, 20 April). Scott rarely missed the national association meetings and commented in his autobiography about encountering many association members during his frequent months in Hot Springs, Arkansas for rest.

The national association was an elite group of progressive businesspeople and entrepreneurs who formed a tremendous network of resources. After visiting the establishments of these various elite businesspeople, Scott "was inspired to spend, in 1932-34, nearly $50,000.00 to renovate [his] places." This renovation illustrates two important points. First, in the mist of the great depression R. C. Scott had the economic resources and confidence to embark on a significant capital rebuilding project. Second, while R. C. Scott successfully beat the local competition in the Richmond market, I contend that he measured his achievements not against A. D. Price, Jr. or Richmond's white funeral directors, but against the national association elite. He viewed his peers as those elite entrepreneurs he met at Hot Springs, Arkansas: the individuals with financial resources also to take off several months each year for rest.

MARKET STRUCTURE

During the first half of the twentieth century, demographic changes restructured the funeral industry. Between 1900 and 1940, the United States' annual population nearly doubled. The population grew from 76,094,000 in 1900 to 132,122,000 by 1940. In contrast, the estimated number of deaths remained consistently between 1.2 million and 1.5 million during those forty years except one year (Illustration 5). Funeral home establishments grew from 16,000 to 40,000 during this 40-year period. Therefore, funeral homes expanded nearer to the rate of the population than to the rate of the deceased. This disparity eventually caused major shifts in the structure of the industry and the way funeral homes conducted business.

Estimates of the U.S. Population

Illustration 5

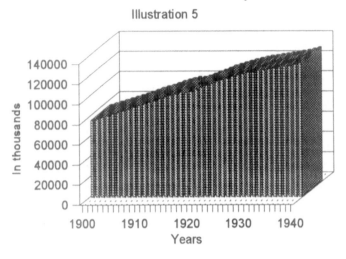

Estimates of the U.S. Deaths

Illustration 6

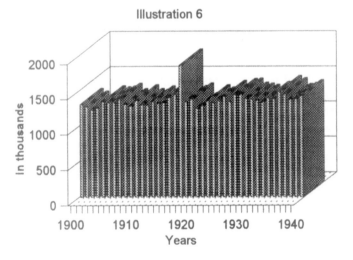

Source: Bureau of the Census 1975. Historical Statistics of
the United States, Colonial Times to 1970, bicentennial
Edition, Part 1 & 2. Washington: U.S. Department of
Commerce.

The economic potential for each establishment diminished as the
number of funeral directors and embalmers grew. In 1900, an average of
82 people died per funeral director. This average dropped to 65 deaths per
funeral director in 1910, 58 deaths per funeral director in 1920, 41 deaths
per funeral director in 1930, and 36 deaths per funeral director in 1940.

U.S. Deaths per Funeral Director

Illustration 7

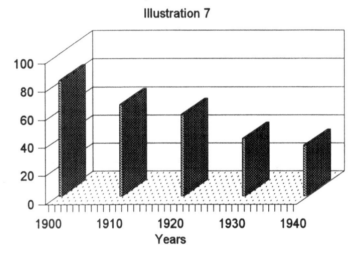

Source: Bureau of the Census 1975. Historical Statistics of
the United States, Colonial Times to 1970, bicentennial
Edition, Part 1 & 2. Washington: U.S. Department of
Commerce.

If we conservatively assume one funeral director per funeral home, the
business practices and financial structure that enabled a funeral home to
survive with 82 clients per year, or three clients every two weeks, was

under tremendous pressure to support a funeral home now serving only 36 clients per year, or two clients every three weeks (Illustration 7). In contrast to the national trends, R. C. Scott "announced an average of slightly over one funeral for each day in 1926" (*Richmond Planet* 1927, 8 January).

Death rates varied for different segments of the population. For instance, the dramatic drop in the infant and children mortalities fueled the declining death rates between 1900 and 1940. This was an important point with funeral directors because they typically priced children's funerals cheaper than adult funerals. Thus, as the ratio of adult funerals to total funerals grew, the funeral director initially experienced higher revenue per burial service (Gebhart 1928, 244). This initial experience probably influenced the industry's decision to overexpand, despite stable United States' death rates. Unfortunately, the higher revenues per funeral did not increase profits, because the absolute number of funerals per funeral home declined rapidly.

America had more funeral establishments than the market could profitably support. This meant the shrinking profit base had to support increasing amounts of overhead per funeral. Leroy Bowman, author of *The American Funeral*, outlined three ways funeral homes responded to the industry restructuring: funerals became more expensive, more lavish, and included more services with undefined value; the profession raised barriers of entry to limit the number of establishments; and the industry installed financial control systems (Bowman 1959, 91).

The rising percentage of adult deaths allowed the funeral director to sell more additional services and to rely less on the sale of paraphernalia. Funeral directors used their new professional status to expand into grief management services (providing flowers, placing ads, filing insurance, supplying chairs, obtaining special funeral clothing, etc.). By the first half of the twentieth century, industry representatives estimated each complete funeral required at least eighty work-hours from the funeral director (Mitford 1963, 64).

While states enacted embalming requirements and required licensing requirements to raise the standards, a look at the state embalming requirements, as of July 1, 1926, suggest that these barriers were low (Table 1). The drive to sell more services and restrict the number of funeral homes through licensing requirements did not help the industry's profitability.

State Embalming Requirements, 1926 Table 1					
States	**Preliminary Education Required**			**Appren-ticeship required**	**Deduct from Appren-ticeship for 26 weeks Course**
	Elem. School	High School	Embalm-ing School		
Alabama	-----	-----	Accepted	2 Yrs.	2 Yrs
Arizona	-----	-----	Accepted	2 Yrs.	1/2 Yr.
Arkansas	-----	-----	Diploma and	1 Yr.	-----
California	-----	-----	Accepted	2 Yrs.	1/2 Yr.
Colorado	-----	-----	Accepted	2 Yrs.	1/2 Yr.
Connecticut	-----	2 Yrs.	Accepted	2 Yrs.	1 Yr.
Delaware	-----	-----	Accepted	1 Yr.	1/2 Yr.
Florida	-----	-----	Accepted	3 Yrs.	3 Yrs.
Georgia	-----	4 Yrs.	Accepted	2 Yrs.	1/2 Yr.
Idaho	-----	4 Yrs.	Accepted	3 Yrs.	1 Yr.
Illinois	8th Grade	-----	Diploma and	1 Yr.	-----
Indiana	-----	4 Yrs.	Accepted	3 Yrs.	3 Yrs.
Iowa	-----	-----	Accepted	2 Yrs.	1 Yr.
Kansas	-----	4 Yrs.	Accepted	3 Yrs.	2 1/2 Yrs.

State Embalming Requirements, 1926 Table 1					
Kentucky	-----	-----	Accepted	3 Yrs.	1/2 Yr.
Louisiana	-----	-----	Accepted	3 Yrs.	2 1/2 Yrs.
Maine	-----	-----	Accepted	1 Yr.	1 Yr.
Maryland	-----	4 Yrs.	Accepted	2 Yrs.	2 Yrs
Massachu-setts	-----	-----	-----	-----	-----
Michigan	-----	2 Yrs.	Accepted	2 Yrs.	1 Yr.
Minnesota	8th Grade	-----	-----	2 Yrs.	1/2 Yr.
Mississippi	-----	-----	Accepted	2 Yrs.	2 Yrs.
Missouri	-----	4 Yrs.	Accepted	2 Yrs.	1/2 Yr.
Montana	-----	-----	Accepted	2 Yrs.	2 Yrs.
Nebraska	8th Grade	-----	Accepted	2 Yrs.	1 Yr.
Nevada	-----	-----	-----	-----	-----
New Hampshire	8th Grade	-----	Diploma and	1 Yr.	-----
New Jersey	-----	-----	-----	2 Yrs.	1/2 year
New Mexico	(1929)	4 Yrs.	Accepted	3 Yrs.	1 1/2 Yrs.
New York	-----	-----	Not Required	-----	-----

State Embalming Requirements, 1926 Table 1					
North Carolina	-----	-----	Accepted	2 Yrs.	1 1/2 Yrs.
North Dakota	-----	4 Yrs.	Diploma and	2 Yrs.	-----
Ohio	-----	4 Yrs.	Diploma and	2 Yrs.	-----
Oklahoma	-----	4 Yrs.	Accepted	2 Yrs.	2 Yrs.
Pennsylvania	-----	-----	Undertaking license only		-----
Rhode Island	-----	-----	-----	-----	-----
South Carolina	-----	-----	Diploma and	1/4 Yr.	-----
South Dakota	-----	-----	Accepted	2 Yrs.	2 Yrs.
Tennessee	-----	-----	Accepted	3 Yrs.	3 Yrs.
Oregon	8th Grade	or	Diploma and	2 Yrs.	1/2 Yr.
Texas	-----	-----	Accepted	2 Yrs.	2 Yrs.
Utah	8th Grade	-----	Accepted	2 Yrs.	1 Yr.
Vermont	-----	-----	-----	-----	-----
Virginia	-----	-----	Accepted	2 Yrs.	1/2 Yr.
Washington	-----	-----	Accepted	2 Yrs.	1 Yr.
West Virginia	-----	4 Yrs.	Accepted	1 Yr.	1/2 Yr.

State Embalming Requirements, 1926 Table 1					
Wisconsin	8th Grade	-----	Accepted	2 Yrs.	Time to be fixed
Wyoming	-----	1 Yr.	Accepted	2 Yrs.	1 Yr.
Dist. of Columbia	-----	-----	Revenue license only		-----

Source: John C. Gebhart. *Funeral Costs: What they Average. Are they too high?* New York-London: Putnam, 1928. 273.

Most firms in the early twentieth century bundled their service charges into the cost of the casket or transportation. Frequently, these charges did not cover the funeral director's cost. Funeral directors could only realize profits from their services, if they could properly charge for them. Few funeral directors could produce an itemized bill listing the price for each specific service or product.

Before 1925, the industry operated without scientific cost accounting. Funeral directors did not have an accounting structure that could accurately allocate their direct or indirect cost to specific functions. Recognizing the potential advantages of a uniformed accounting system, two national associations of funeral directors (the National Funeral Directors' Association and the National Selected Morticians) jointly sponsored a uniform cost-accounting study in 1925. By September 1926, a pilot group of eighteen funeral homes, including the largest and most progressive ones, tracked six hundred funeral transactions using a uniform cost accounting system.

The funeral directors broke-even or made a profit in only 53 percent of the 600 funeral transactions studied. They identified only 10 percent of the transactions that produced excessive profits. Most of the losses resulted from infant funerals and handling bodies shipped from other locations (Gebhart 1928, 243). A faulty pricing system produced the consistent losses on children's funerals. Typically, most funeral directors set adult prices based on the cost of the selected casket. They priced a complete adult funeral at three to six times the cost of the casket (Bowman 1959, 46). The charge for an infant or child's funeral was traditionally smaller than an adult funeral charge. Because only a slight cost differential, if any, existed between the cost of the two caskets, the payment for a child's funeral rarely covered the overhead. Whether funeral directors charged low fees for children's funerals because few children had insurance or because of their own belief that it was the right thing to do, they consistently lost money on these funerals.

A faulty pricing program also contributed to the consistent losses associated with burying bodies shipped from other locations. The casket price usually covered the payment for services. Therefore, when bodies arrived in caskets, the sending funeral directors received most of the family's payment for services in the casket payment. The receiving funeral directors usually refused to charge an appropriate price for their services, thus guaranteeing financial losses.

The pricing policy of funeral directors created controversy both in and out of the industry. Wilbur Krieger, author of several books on funeral management, Managing Director of the National Selected Morticians, Inc. and Director of the National Foundation of Funeral Service stated:

> bring 10 or 1,000 funeral directors together, give them all the same set of cost factors, and probably no two of them will arrive at the same selling price. Neither will they follow the same procedure in reaching their respective selling prices. (Krieger 1951, 258)

This lack of consistency obstructed most profit figure calculations for the industry.

Unlike the industry's vague financial picture, one can figure out the prices charged to consumers by analyzing the wholesale value of burial merchandise. Table 2 illustrates the "Growth of the Manufacture and Wholesale Value of Burial Goods" over sixty-six years. Before 1890, small, neighborhood suppliers dominated the industry. Few undertakers bought complete caskets in this early period. The large number of establishments, but low average wholesale cost per funeral exemplified this point. In the next stage of industry development, the wholesale value of burial goods rose from $12.2 million in 1889 to $70.4 million in 1925, despite the constant number of deaths during the period. The average wholesale cost per funeral rose from $10.11 to $51.89 in the same period. One can attribute part of the price increase to the general rise in wholesale prices experienced by the United States from 1893 until the start of World War I. However, after using price indexes to correct for inflation, the corrected wholesale value of burial goods in 1925 was $25.94. This amount still registered an increase of 150 percent (Gebhart 1928, 224). Assuming the funeral homes wanted at least to break even financially, and thus passed on the wholesale cost increases, the public experienced higher cost in the first quarter of the twentieth century both on a relative and absolute basis. If the funeral directors wanted a profit or income to offset their declining number of clients, then the public's funeral expenditures were even larger.

Growth of the Manufacture and Wholesale Value of Burial Goods (Coffins, Caskets, Embalming Supplies, clothing, Etc.) From 1859 to 1925, From Data Collected by the United States Census of Manufactures
Table 2

Year	No. of Estab- lish- ments	No. of Wage Earners	Avg. Number of Wage Earners	Total Vol. of Bus. (000's)	Est. No. of Annual Deaths (000's)	Avg. Whole- sale Cost per Funeral
1859	210	688	3.3	$1,025	639	$1.60*
1869	642	2,365	3.7	4,027	771	5.22
1879	769	4,415	5.7	8,158	969	8.42
1889	194	5,751	29.6	12,231	1,210	10.11
1899	217	6,840	31.5	13,952	1,341	10.41
1904	239	8,468	35.4	20,266	1,361	14.89
1909	284	9,339	32.9	24,526	1,372	17.88
1914	287	9,468	33.9	26,325	1,344	19.58
1919	351	11,890	33.9	64,377	1,352	47.62
1921	314	9,956	31.7	54,796	1,225	44.71
1923	327	11,593	35.5	65,558	1,369	47.89
1925	326	11,479	35.2	70,413	1,357	51.89

*Monetary items in depreciation. Currency in gold approximately 80 per cent of its nominal value.
Source: John C. Gebhart. *Funeral Costs: What they Average. Are they too high?* New York-London: Putnam, 1928. 223.

The rising funeral bills caused the clergy, intellectuals, and social workers continuously to question and attack the large expenditures Americans spent on death rituals. They correctly pointed out that the dollar amounts were large in comparison to the cost of basic human day-to-day needs. Yet, compared with the expense of the other major sacred rite-of-passage ceremony that families financed; the wedding, funeral expenditures appear reasonable. People paid, on average, twice the amount for a wedding than they would for a funeral (Fulton 1961, 317-23). In addition, families incurred these higher wedding expenditures without the benefit of insurance. When looking at sacred ceremonies financed by the family, one must recognize that these ceremonies satisfy a cultural status need, and most consumers find it inappropriate to judge these ceremonies using economic rationalization.

ETHNIC-BASED DEATH RITUALS

Society, or more specifically ethnic groups within the society, dictate appropriate funeral expenditures based on class and status. Ethnic-based death rituals allowed funeral directors to structure their business along ethnic lines. They could construct cultural barriers that protected their ethnic client base. A short review of Jewish and Italian death customs illustrates the specific ethnic demands placed upon funeral directors.

According to orthodox Jewish tradition, a dead body was ritually unclean; however, to purge the body of its impurities, a holy society conducted an intricate scrubbing ritual, called the Tahara. Embalming was forbidden. After the Tahara, someone dressed the body in a simple linen shroud. Under this tradition Jewish people viewed death as uncomplicated and the entire funeral was unadorned and unpretentious. They preferred a simple unpolished wood coffin. A black cloth usually draped the coffin. Often, the burial occurred within twenty-four hours (Gebhart 1928, 9).

In the traditional Italian funeral, family and friends bought seats in the horse-drawn funeral carriage for the immediate surviving family. They paid the money directly to the family. Since families received several times the actual cost of the seats, it was a way to provide financial support to the surviving family. By the twentieth century, this tradition evolved into a custom of simply presenting the surviving family with money at the funeral. The surviving family had total discretion over the money. They typically used the money to meet funeral expenses or to create a benefaction in the memory of the departed. Thus, the "funeral was a gift

received and given by both the deceased and those who survived him"
(Galante 1976, 143). Flowers played a prominent role in the Italian
funeral. The funeral director routinely provided additional flower cars to
transport the large number of flowers to the cemetery. These flower cars
added to the funeral procession. The funeral procession itself held great
significance in the Italian community. Commonly the family required the
procession to drive past the home or the decease's place of business.

On the surface, the Italian, Jewish, and African American funerals
looked entirely different and encompassed many diverse rituals and
customs, but most funeral directors had the necessary skills to conduct any
of these funerals. Yet, funeral directors preferred to conduct funerals in
a narrow, predictable realm. Their anxiety over making a mistake
performing an outside funeral kept most funeral homes from having an
ethnically diverse client base. A prominent exception was in rural areas
where only one funeral home existed, and the literature does not suggest
that these firms faced any special difficulties. Even today, the trade
directories identify African American funeral homes by race. This keeps
funeral homes from inadvertently shipping a white body to an African
American funeral home (Bowman 1959, 95). This is not to insinuate that
only funeral directors support the ethnic segregation of funerals. If a
family has a choice of funeral homes, most families select the funeral home
supporting their ethnic group (Federal Trade Commission 1977, 18) to
reduce the same anxiety.

GOVERNMENT REGULATION

In the United States, the funeral industry engaged in a two-tier
relationship with the government. They lobbied the state for assistance to
legitimize their trade and erect barriers to entry, but they also staunchly
opposed any type of public regulation of their services. The funeral
industry's opposition to government regulation postponed the imposition of
funeral service regulations in America until the late 1970s. The
government finally intervened because its studies showed that families were
at a distinct disadvantage when conducting commercial transactions with
a profit-motivated funeral director. They contended that the disadvantage
resulted from the family's emotional state (Federal Trade Commission
1977, 23).

Mandated price disclosures were the primary feature of the 1978
Federal Trade Commission funeral industry regulations.

> In selling or offering to sell funeral goods or funeral services
> to the public, it is an unfair or deceptive act or practice for
> a funeral provider to fail to furnish price information
> disclosing the cost to the purchaser for each of the specific
> funeral goods and funeral services used in connection with
> the disposition of deceased human bodies, including at least
> the price of embalming, transportation of remains, use of
> facilities, caskets, outer burial containers, immediate burials,
> or direct cremations, to persons inquiring about the purchase
> of funerals. (Federal Trade Commission 1978, 294)

The government realized that the inconsistent pricing structure, outlined earlier, had the potential to exploit the consumer. Funeral directors quoted different prices for the same unmarked item based on how they sized up the consumer.

Officials warned the industry as early as 1923 that their business practices, especially price bundling, were an invitation for government intervention. The Casket Manufacturers' Association of America sponsored a conference specifically to consider uneconomical and unethical practices in the burial industry. Lee K. Frankel, the second vice-president of Metropolitan Life Insurance Company, made the following remarks in an address to the conference:

> What will happen if the public continues to maintain the
> impression, incorrectly though this may be, that many
> funeral directors are taking advantage of a situation which
> arises at the time of death, to the detriment of the relatives of
> the deceased? I have no desire to appear as an alarmist, but
> I feel fairly confident, looking ahead, that unless funeral
> directors readjust their business, the time will come when
> there will be intervention on the part of Government . . . this
> has already taken place to a remarkable degree in many of
> the important communities in Europe, particularly the city of
> Frankfort in Germany and in certain cantons of Switzerland.
> (Gebhart 1928, xiv)

The American funeral industry was a product of the social and economic changes experienced by the United States at the beginning of the twentieth century. In America, the funeral industry achieved a level of commercialization unparalleled in Europe. The government never played a role in early American burials except as a provider of pauper and military funerals. Americans avoided looking to the government for help. The lowest segments of American society took great pride in not needing government burials (Borchert 1980, 139). American society's devotion to the private market gave the funeral industry a unique level of political and economic power. Funeral directors used this power to thwart governmental intrusion into their business practices and to remain a uniquely American industry.

DO THE POOR PAY MORE?

> There is strong conviction throughout the funeral directors'
> group that a family should arrange for a funeral on the level
> of its capacity to pay. This conviction is freely expressed by
> individual undertakers, by the booklets put out to attract
> patronage, by the funeral directors' associations in their
> publications, by the independent trade journals, by cemetery
> officials, and by florists. This concept forms the basis for
> court decisions on the allowable amounts of estate funds
> usable for burial purposes. Funeral directors defend the
> concept based on the dual assumption that according to the
> accepted customs: (1) a family should spend a sum and
> present a display appropriate to its status, and (2) the love
> and respect of the family for its dead is shown to the world
> by the funeral in terms of money spent. They express
> disbelief, disgust, or violent disapproval of standards
> contrary in effect to their assumptions. (Bowman 1959, 47)

The ethical nature of these transactions only comes into question if pricing does not follow cost, and if pricing does not adjust down and up based on the client's economic means. If the poor paid a disproportionately high price for burial services, either the funeral directors used their pricing philosophy to extract additional surplus profits, or the poor place a higher value on obtaining status through funerals.

In May 1926, The Advisory Committee on Burial Survey conducted an independent study of burial customs and costs. John C. Gebhart wrote the final report and set out to answer two central questions. First, what did funerals cost? Second, did funeral charges fall with undue severity upon those least able to pay? The committee made painstaking efforts to collect data on funeral cost. Their statistical research has no peer.

The committee sought to secure funeral costs for typical communities and distinct economic groups. They analyzed fifteen thousand and one hundred funeral bills obtained from the following sources:

2,830	decedents' estates in New York, Brooklyn, Chicago and Pittsburgh,
8,828	industrial policyholders from various sections of the United States,
3,123	claims for burial expenses filed with the United States Veterans Bureau, and
319	widows who applied for pensions from the New York Board of Child Welfare.

15,100

The Metropolitan Life Insurance Company sponsored the study with an initial $25,000 appropriation. In the early 1900s, Metropolitan Life received negative reports from social workers and charitable agencies about certain funeral directors serving low-income clients. The reports accused these funeral directors of soliciting the value of their clients' insurance policies and charging that figure for funeral expenses. Metropolitan Life's inability to establish the average cost of a "decent" funeral from funeral industry sources led them to initiate the study. Metropolitan worked to insure that the committee was independent and conducted an unbiased analysis. The Advisory Committee on Burial Survey incorporated representatives from different sections of the country, with various religious backgrounds from leading professions, including funeral directors.

Analyzing estates provides cross sections of a community's economic groups and the burial cost associated with those economic groups. Clarence B. Metzger asserted in *Contributions of Life Insurance Research to the Estate Problem* that estates typically existed for 25 to 30 percent of the adults that died. These estates usually extended throughout all the economic groups (Metzger 1925, Gebhart 1928, 69). While difficulties may arise when comparing two cities, this resource gives an accurate view of burial expenses and economic groups in any particular community where the records exist. When difficulties arise, they are usually from inconsistent definitions and different estate information requirements.

New York
When looking at the estates in Manhattan (New York County) versus those in Brooklyn (Kings County), the wealth of Manhattan is apparent (Table 3).

Distribution of Estates, New York and Kings Counties, 1926 Table 3a						
Value of Estates	New York County			Kings County		
	No.	Per Cent	Cum. Per Cent	No	Per Cent	Cum. Per Cent
Under $1000	17	1.7	1.7	23	2.7	2.7
1,000- 4,999	192	19.7	21.4	188	21.7	24.4
5,000- 9,999	154	15.8	37.2	230	26.6	51.0
10,000- 29,999	224	23.0	60.2	247	28.5	79.5
30,000- 49,999	82	8.4	68.6	73	8.4	87.9
50,000- 99,999	115	11.8	80.4	61	7.0	94.9
100,000-499,999	136	14.0	94.4	38	4.4	99.3
500,000-999,999	28	2.9	97.3	4	.5	99.8
1,000,000 and over	26	2.7	100.0	2	.2	100.0
Total	974	100.0		866	100.0	

Distribution of Estates, New York and Kings Counties, 1926 Table 3b			
Value of Estates	New York and Kings Counties		
	No.	Per Cent	Cum. Per Cent
Under $1000	40	2.2	2.2
1,000– 4,999	380	20.6	22.8
5,000– 9,999	384	20.9	43.7
10,000– 29,999	471	25.6	69.3
30,000– 49,999	155	8.4	77.7
50,000– 99,999	176	9.6	87.3
100,000–499,999	174	9.5	96.8
500,000–999,999	32	1.7	98.5
1,000,000 and over	28	1.5	100.0
Total	1,840	100	

Source: John C. Gebhart. *Funeral Costs: What they Average. Are they too high?* New York-London: Putnam, 1928. 72.

Estates valued at less than $10,000 make up 51 percent of the estates in Brooklyn, while in Manhattan they make up only 37.2 percent of the estates Gebhart identified. However, the Manhattan data presents a more accurate picture of funeral expenses segmented by the various economic groups because of the large quantity and even distribution of estates throughout the economic scale. Whether analyzing the percentage of gross or net estates spent on funerals, table 4 illustrates that burial expenses did not have a proportional impact on different economic groups.[1] The 192 estates identified with values between $1000 and $5000 reported an average funeral charge of $541.21. This charge consumed on average 23.7

---

[1] Net estates are defined as an estate where all debts and administrative expenses except the burial expenses and taxes were deducted.

percent of their net estate and 18.6 percent of the gross estate.

Distribution of New York County Estates by Size Showing Per Cent of Net and Gross Estates Expended for Funerals, 1926 Table 4				
Value of Estates	Total Number of Estates	Funeral and Burial Expenses		
		Average Amount	Per Cent of Net Estate	Per Cent of Gross Estate
Under $1000	17	$ 371.83	61.7	52.2
1,000- 4,999	192	541.21	23.7	18.6
5,000- 9,999	154	673.79	11.0	9.1
10,000- 29,999	224	864.55	5.7	5.0
30,000- 49,999	82	1,015.61	3.1	2.7
50,000- 99,999	115	1,080.71	1.8	1.5
100,000-499,999	136	1,961.49	1.0	.9
500,000-999,999	28	2,693.37	.5	.4
1,000,000 and over	26	3,075.42	.2	.2
Total	974	$1,065.05		

Source: John C. Gebhart. *Funeral Costs: What they Average. Are they too high?* New York-London: Putnam, 1928. 74.

The 17 estates valued under $1,000 used 61.7 percent of their net estate and 52.2 percent of the gross estate for funeral expenses. For the 21.4 percent of the New York estates valued below $5,000, the economic burden on their survivors appears substantial compared with the next level of economic groups.

Separating the burial expenses charged by auxiliary enterprises from the estate records is a problem when attempting to deriving specific funeral director charges. When the researcher can separate the basic funeral expenses from auxiliary charges, the separation creates an opportunity to compare an average set of services with a more simple "decent" burial. Gebhart segregated the New York county extra charges into three categories: monuments and mausoleums, cemetery plots and perpetual care, and flowers. A list of these charges appears in table 5. By combining these isolated extra charges (Table 5) with the percentage of estates spent on funerals (Table 4), the data revealed how different economic subcultures defined socially acceptable standards for burial customs (Table 6).

"Extra" Charges in Various New York County Estates 1926 Table 5a				
Value of Estates	Total Number of Estates	Monuments and Mausoleums ($25 and Over)		
		No. of Cases	Per Cent. of Total	Average Charge
Under $1000	17	2	11.8	$ 193.00
1,000- 4,999	192	38	19.8	231.05
5,000- 9,999	154	47	30.5	346.36
10,000- 29,999	224	76	33.9	460.95
30,000- 49,999	82	23	28.0	534.43
50,000- 99,999	115	36	31.3	543.97
100,000-499,999	136	53	39.0	1,516.02
500,000-999,999	28	11	39.3	1,902.91
1,000,000 and over	26	12	46.2	1,844.33
Total	974	298	30.6	$ 729.21

"Extra" Charges in Various New York County Estates 1926 Table 5b				
Value of Estates	Total Number of Estates	Cemetery Plots and Pertetual Care ($150 and Over)		
		No. of Cases	Per Cent. of Total	Average Charge
Under $1000	17			
1,000- 4,999	192	5	2.6	$ 237.00
5,000- 9,999	154	11	7.1	340.27
10,000- 29,999	224	16	7.1	531.19
30,000- 49,999	82	5	6.1	444.20
50,000- 99,999	115	4	3.5	605.00
100,000-499,999	136	15	11.0	1,532.33
500,000-999,999	28	3	10.7	3,897.33
1,000,000 and over	26	1	3.8	2,500.00
Total	974	60	6.2	$ 920.75

	Total Number of Estates	Flowers ($25 and Over)		
Value of Estates		No. of Cases	Per Cent. of Total	Average Charge
Under $1000	17			
1,000- 4,999	192	1	.5	$ 395.00
5,000- 9,999	154	2	1.3	53.00
10,000- 29,999	224	1	.4	291.00
30,000- 49,999	82	2	2.4	460.00
50,000 -99,999	115	4	3.5	312.50
100,000-499,999	136	8	5.9	335.13
500,000-999,999	28	3	10.7	1,214.33
1,000,000 and over	26	5	19.2	772.20
Total	974	26	2.7	$ 505.65

"Extra" Charges in Various New York County Estates
1926
Table 5c

Source: John C. Gebhart. *Funeral Costs: What they Average. Are they too high?* New York-London: Putnam, 1928. 77.

Table 6 displays, according to the value of estates, the separation of average burial expense growth versus the growth of extra charges. In the smaller estates, the extra charges are a very small part of the funeral expenses. However, as the estates increased in value, suggesting a higher level of wealth, the survivors chose to spend a proportionally higher amount on monuments and their cemetery plots than on the actual funeral service. Gebhart explains this phenomenon among the wealthy as the "family complex" at work. The "family complex" is:

expressed in a desire to perpetuate the family name in stone
and in well-cared-for burial plots. The funeral, while
dignified and by no means cheap, is relatively of less
importance than among lower-income groups. With poorer
groups the interest is perhaps most ephemeral and is centered
in a "fine funeral" to show respect to the dead and to impress
curious neighbors. (Gebhart 1928, 80)

What Gebhart fails to recognize in his analysis is that the family complex
is not an option for lower-income groups.

Burial Expenses and "Net" Funeral Bill of Estates in New York County, 1926 — Table 6a				
Value of Estates	Total Number of Estates	Average Burial Expense	Average "Extra" Charges	Per Cent. of Total Burial Expense
Under $1000	17	$ 371.83	$ 22.70	6.1
1,000 -4,999	192	541.21	53.96	10.0
5,000- 9,999	154	673.79	131.35	19.5
10,000- 29,999	224	864.55	195.63	22.6
30,000- 49,999	82	1,015.61	188.21	18.5
50,000 -99,999	115	1,080.71	214.72	19.9
100,000-499,999	136	1,961.49	779.52	39.7
500,000-999,999	28	2,693.37	1,295,25	48.1
1,000,000 and over	26	3,075.42	1,095.89	35.6
Total	974	$1,065.05	$ 293.33	27.5

| Burial Expenses and "Net" Funeral Bill of Estates in New York County, 1926 Table 6b | | | | |
Value of Estates	Total Number of Estates	"Net" Funeral Bill	Per Cent. of Net Estate	Per Cent. of Gross Estate
Under $1000	17	$ 349.13	57.9	49.0
1,000- 4,999	192	487.25	21.3	16.8
5,000- 9,999	154	542.44	8.9	7.3
10,000- 29,999	224	668.92	4.6	3.9
30,000- 49,999	82	827.40	2.5	2.2
50,000- 99,999	115	865.99	1.4	1.2
100,000-499,999	136	1,181.97	.6	.5
500,000-999,999	28	1,398.12	.2	.2
1,000,000 and over	26	1,979.53	.1	.1
Total	974	$ 771.73		

Source: John C. Gebhart. *Funeral costs: What they Average. Are they too high?* New York-London: Putnam, 1928. 79.

The major expenses in funeral services were the embalming procedures, the casket, and burial plot. Embalming and caskets were basic and consistent expenditures for most funerals no matter the family's income levels. After these basic expenses, families chose the category of additional funeral expenses based on economic status. Lower economic groups incurred most of their additional funeral expenses outside the estate's purview. These expenditures went toward the funeral feast, clothing, travel, and photographers. They concentrated on the immediate celebration of death. The upper income groups chose to spend their additional funeral money on a beautiful cemetery plot and imposing monuments. These items created both status symbols for the wealthy and cultural barriers to the lower-income and minority ethnic groups. Lower-income groups did not have the option of spending their money on monuments and cemeteries. African Americans and other ethnic groups had very restricted access to cemeteries. Locked out of the high status cemeteries, circumstances did not encourage them to build major monuments in their designated cemeteries. Permanent access to a plot was rare in African American or municipal cemeteries. African-Americans saw their caskets frequently reburied, doubled stacked or exposed to vandals. Such insecure conditions offered little incentive for the lower-income client to spend money in the cemetery. They preferred to spend money on the actual event of the funeral.

Chicago

Estate records gathered from Cook County (Chicago) had three distinct features from the New York estates: the funeral costs consisted of funeral director charges without the extra items; the county defined estates as personal property only; and the probate court took a proactive stance against legal and funeral expenses decimating small estates. Cook County's probate court routinely disallowed funeral charges it judged "excessive." The court did not hesitate to force the funeral director to absorb what it considered excessive charge.

While the different definitions of estate and funeral charges limit direct comparison between New York and Chicago, the even distribution of estates along economic lines permits a valid look into the Chicago community (Table 7). The court judged 30 funeral bills among the 524 analyzed as "excessive." Two-thirds of the reduced bills were for estates under $2000 and the reduction averaged 34.9 percent (Table 8). The study identified an additional 104 estates under review at the time of the study. These contested cases appear next to the approved 524 estates in table 9. Most of the 104 contested funeral bills were from estates valued under $4,000 and their alleged excess over the approved bills was 37.5 percent. The outcome of the contested bills is unknown but the court presents enough data to show what the courts and heirs in Chicago considered excessive.

Distribution of Estates by Size and Average Funeral Bill, Cook County (Chicago), Illinois, 1926 Table 7			
Value of Estates (Personal Property only)	Number	Per Cent. of Total Number	Average Funeral Bill
Under $2,000	188	35.9	$339.26
2,000-9,999	164	31.3	439.51
10,000 and over	172	32.8	672.99
Total	524	100.0	$480.18

Source: John C. Gebhart. *Funeral costs: What they Average. Are they too high?* New York-London: Putnam, 1928. 88.

Average Amounts Claimed and Allowed for Funeral Expenses in Estates of Various Amounts, Cook County (Chicago), Illinois 1926 Table 8					
Value of Estates (Personal Property only)	No.	Avg. Amount Claimed	Avg. Amount Allowed	Avg. Reduc- tion	Per Cent. of Amount Claimed
Under $500	6	$485.11	$320.14	$164.97	34.0
500- 999	4	454.02	231.00	223.02	49.1
1,000- 1,999	10	450.76	270.35	180.41	40.0
2,000- 2,999	3	611.68	370.00	241.68	39.5
5,000- 9,999	3	587.07	276.69	310.38	52.9
10,000-29,999	4	977.81	851.43	126.37	12.9
Total	30	$558.06	$363.13	$194.93	34.9

Source: John C. Gebhart. *Funeral Costs: What they Average. Are they too high?* New York-London: Putnam, 1928. 89.

The average amount of overcharges is not as important as the number of cases. Out of the 628 estates reviewed, the court cited 134, or 21 percent, for being excessive. Despite the court's opposition to large charges in small estates, the county's funeral directors still submitted enough large bills for the court to reject one out of every five.

Value of Estates	Approved Funeral Bills	
	No.	Average Amount
Real Estate Only	3	$ 553.42
Under $500	57	328.69
500- 999	55	319.02
1,000- 1,999	73	353.96
2,000- 2,999	46	390.54
3,000- 3,999	27	468.93
4,000 -4,999	27	451.11
5,000- 9,999	64	457.40
10,000- 29,000	92	566.10
30,000- 49,000	23	592.69
50,000- 99,000	23	590.78
100,000-499,999	27	911.15
500,000-999,999	4	1,267.80
1,000,000 and over	3	2,260.25
Total	524	$ 480.18

Approved Undertakers' Bills
Cook County (Chicago), Illinois, 1926
Table 9a

Contested Undertakers' Bills Cook County (Chicago), Illinois, 1926 Table 9b				
Value of Estates	Contested Funeral Bills			
	No	Average Amount	Excess Over Approved Bills	
			Amount	Per Cent
Real Estate Only	1	$ 326.80	$126.92	22.9
Under $500	11	447.35	118.66	36.1
500- 999	11	520.01	201.59	63.2
1,000- 1,999	12	503.15	149.19	42.1
2,000- 2,999	12	551.35	160.81	41.2
3,000- 3,999	9	601.61	132.68	28.3
4,000- 4,999	7	715.73	264.62	58.7
5,000- 9,999	14	852.56	395.16	86.4
10,000- 29,000	19	576.28	10.18	1.8
30,000- 49,000	2	510.88	181.81	30.7
50,000- 99,000	4	628.46	37.68	6.4
100,000-499,999	2	4,095.83	3,184.68	349.5
500,000-999,999				
1,000,000 and over				
Total	104	$ 660.24	$ 180.06	37.5

Source: John C. Gebhart. *Funeral Costs: What they Average. Are they too high?* New York-London: Putnam, 1928. 91

Since the evidence suggests that the probate court reviewed most filing, especially those valued below $10,000, the funeral directors routinely assumed the risk of losing money on each of these cases. There had to be circumstances that compelled the funeral directors to charge small estates these "excessive" fees, especially when the court consistently rejected the fees. I believe class conflict more than poor business judgment explains the discrepancy. If one assumes that all these cases were legitimate commercial transactions, where the funeral director simply provided the services demanded, then what the data reveals are the imposition of middle-class values on lower-class social customs. Were the courts punishing the lower class for selecting funeral rituals that focused upon an immediate glorification and celebration of death, versus the aristocratic and socially acceptable long-term death rituals that emphasized cemetery plots and monuments? If lower class, ethnic mourning customs were different because of cultural preferences, then one can view the probate courts' actions as mainstream society prejudging lower-income funeral behavior as 'deviant'.

Insurance Policies

Gebhart developed national average burial costs by analyzing death claims from 8,828 industrial insurance policies. These Metropolitan Life Insurance policies have several limitations. People typically had more than one insurance policy and the characteristics of Metropolitan Life's customers versus all industrial insurance policy holders are unknown. However, by 1926, insurance was the "financial life blood of funeral homes" according to R. C. Scott's autobiography.

Listed in table 10 and table 11 are the average costs of 7,871 adult burials by states and 2,765 adult burials by selected cities, respectively. Recorded separately in table 12 are burial costs for children under twelve. The tables illustrate a tremendous variation of funeral cost throughout the country. For example, in New Jersey, Pennsylvania, Massachusetts, Ohio and New York funeral costs were more than twice the average cost of a burial in North Carolina.

Adult Funeral Cost for 7,871 Industrial Policyholders February 7, 1927-June 30, 1927 Table 10					
States	Number of Adult Deaths	Average Cost of Burial	States	Number of Adult Deaths	Average Cost of Burial
NJ	563	$483.82	KS	100	279.28
PA	917	442.25	DC	131	258.69
MA	218	422.18	TN	200	251.90
OH	106	414.74	MD	255	244.81
NY	1844	403.76	KY	244	232.84
MI	368	380.26	VA	122	226.23
IL	992	369.58	GA	95	220.32
IN	186	323.15	LA	194	218.09
MO	591	309.76	NC	114	194.13
			18 Other States	631	325.83
			Total	7871	$363.13

Source: *Funeral Costs: What They Average. Are They Too High?* New York-London: Putnam, 1928. 274.

Adult Funeral Cost for 2,765 Industrial Policyholders April 15, 1927-June 30, 1927 Table 11		
Cities	Number of Adult Deaths	Average Cost of Burial
Newark	68	$493.19
Philadelphia	323	483.20
New York	883	431.53
Cleveland	71	403.00
Detroit	197	391.95
Chicago	591	380.83
St. Louis	237	351.43
Baltimore	107	248.93
Louisville	76	237.70
Nashville	59	233.49
Five Other Cities*	153	378.14

* Buffalo, Indianapolis, Milwaukee, Atlanta and Boston.
Source: *Funeral Costs: What They Average. Are They Too High?* New York-London: Putnam, 1928. 275.

The cost of children's funerals highlights the unsophisticated pricing policies discussed earlier in the book. The cost for an average child's funeral was 63 percent less than the cost for an average adult funeral. Because overhead and embalming costs were the same and children's caskets were not appreciably cheaper, imagining that the funeral director's adult funeral expenses were 63 percent higher than those experienced in childrens' funerals is hard (Table 10 and Table 12). Since most children did not have insurance and few left behind estates, the lower prices probably appeared fair to the community. However, the lower price for children's funerals consistently generated loses because the charges could not cover the full burial cost.

Funeral Cost for 957 Children Under Twelve Years of Age February 7, 1927-June 30, 1927 Table 12		
States	Number of Deaths	Average Cost of Burial
New York	247	$193.51
Pennsylvania	95	141.62
Massachusetts	49	139.24
New Jersey	72	137.40
Michigan	75	118.39
Illinois	142	106.42
28 Other States	277	96.20
Total	957	$134.39

Source: *Funeral Costs: What They Average. Are They Too High?* New York-London: Putnam, 1928. 275.

Gebhart discovered three tendencies in his research on industrial policies: funeral expenses were highest in the north and eastern sections of the country; the larger cities had higher burial expenses; and the cost differential between adult and children funerals appeared unreasonable.

Gebhart's examination of 3,123 death claims at the Veteran's Bureau provided better access to the medium, small, and rural communities than the industrial insurance policy data. The Veteran Bureau material yields information on all types of communities in the United States. The Veteran cases verified the connection of higher burial cost and higher population densities. Gebhart reasoned that burial expenses varied with the size of the city because land values, wages, rents, and taxes increase as cities become larger. I argue that the increased expenditures were the high cost of obtaining status when few people personally know the survivor's economic standing. As people became socially isolated and nameless entities in the crowded urban environments, they needed higher expenditures to acquire their desired status.

The Committee on Burial Survey looked at the burial expenditures of dependent widows in New York, but only studied a random sample of 319 records. This data produced inconclusive results.

SUMMARY

The history of American burial customs is a history of the historical and cultural transformations in the United States. As the people involved in the undertaking trade organized into a profession, they used technology and industrialization to provide more sophisticated services for their clients. Their inconsistent pricing policy created financial instability in the industry and public debate over the value of their services. This debate continues today. How does society decide the proper cost of funeral services? Should market-value, government regulation, or cultural status determine what makes a 'decent funeral' and what it should cost?

III
The Origin of African American Death and Mourning Rituals

INTRODUCTION

Culture is not a fixed condition but a process: the product
of interaction between the past and present. Its toughness
and resiliency are determined not by a culture's ability to
withstand change, which indeed may be a sign of stagnation
not life, but by its ability to react creatively and responsively
to the realities of a new situation. (Levine 1977, 5)

Many scholarly methods are incapable of revealing the interesting
details of African American culture because they depend on elite writing
and legal documents. As scholars begin using traditional research tools
such as folk expressions (Levine 1977, 5), music (Baker 1984, Cone
1972), and material culture (Thompson 1983), African-Americans from the
eighteenth and early nineteenth century become more historically
articulate. This study advocates that the best tool for analyzing culture is
an examination of ritual behavior. The Durkheim school argues that rituals
are the primary technique a society uses to maintain its unity. Ritual acts
create and perpetuate the social system (Fishbane 1989, 65). Among ritual
acts, funeral rituals are prime examples.

Emile Durkheim's theory of rituals, published in his 1915 book
Elementary Forms of the Religious Life, is still the theoretical foundation
for the study of death and mourning rituals. Many sociologists agree with
Durkheim (Radcliffe-Brown 1952, Hertz 1960, and Douglas 1973, 1975,
1979) that rituals are a primary means of social control (Fishbane 1989,
66). Rituals maintain a common belief system through collective action.
The most recent work of Barry Schwartz (1991), Simcha Fishbane (1989),
and Victor Turner (1969, 1974) expands the power of rituals beyond the
limits suggested by Durkheim.

MOURNING RITUALS

Human beings are the only members of the animal kingdom that can anticipate their own death and the potential extinction of their species. No other animals can plan their lives or their individual actions with future death as one determinant. This very ability to anticipate death is a source of feelings of meaningfulness and uselessness, anxiety and love, resignation and denial, achievement and failure. It generates poetry and art and music and building and conquest and deceit and delusion and pain. Death can have heroic size or pitiful smallness, perhaps in direct relationship to our perception of the heroism or pettiness of life. (Kalish and Reynolds 1981, 1)

Society's unique relationships with death and rituals are cornerstones of Emile Durkheim's research into the origin and nature of religion (Durkheim 1915). His general conclusion that religion and morality are not individualistic beliefs but products of collective thoughts or social circumstances provide the theoretical foundation for his studies of mourning and funeral rites. Durkheim asserts in his study of peculiar rites that "one initial fact is constant: mourning is not the spontaneous expression of individual emotions" (Durkheim 1915, 442). Mourning rites are not solely or primarily expressions of individual grief as defined by Durkheim. When a person experiences true grief over the loss of a loved one, publicly exposing this raw sentiment does little to soothe the individual's agitated emotions. Mourning rituals are conventions imposed by the community.

Durkheim argues that when mourners beat themselves, lacerate themselves, burn themselves, and even submit to torture, the mourning ritual obviously satisfies a greater community function:

When someone dies, the family group to which he belongs feels itself lessened and to react against this loss, it assembles. A common misfortune has the same effect as the approach of a happy event; collective sentiments are renewed which then lead men to seek one another and to assemble. (Durkheim 1915, 445)

Funerals provide a forum for mourners to cluster. This clustering is similar to the effect of natural disasters such as hurricanes, fires, floods, or mud-slides. These natural events show no discrimination; everybody is vulnerable, and the community, once equalized, pulls together to confront the common calamity and generate mutual consolation. The difference between mutual consolation during a funeral and during a natural disaster is the presence of ceremony in the funeral. Durkheim asserts that funeral rites are a structural way to bring the community together and reaffirm interdependencies and cultural bonds. Mourning rites incorporating pain, torture, etc. are methods to bring nongrieving members into collective, community mourning and sharing. As the community gathers and displays collective grief, it lifts a burden off the immediate family. The community reassures the family of its place in the society, despite the loss of one of their connections through death.

Hertz and Douglas modernize Durkheim's theories but reaffirm his general thesis. Hertz concentrates on the individual survivor within the community. According to Fishbane, Hertz's basic hypothesis says,

> mourning rites are concerned with the resocialization (whether psychological, or sociological) of the individual survivor as well as the body and soul of the deceased. The rituals concerned with death have a latent function: the intense emotions of individuals are socialized; that which had the potential for social disruption is channeled in communally approved directions. (Fishbane 1989, 66)

Douglas bypasses investigating rituals as resocialization for individual survivors or as an event to reaffirm interdependencies. She analyzes rituals as society's tool for social control:

> One may perceive the "group's" exploitation of rituals as a means of implicitly conveying to the member its message of communal authority, and thus reinforcing the boundaries of the society. Therefore, mourning rites, an example of a ritual process performed within a group structure, serve to strengthen the group norms. (Fishbane 1989, 67)

While Hertz and Douglas do not address specifically African American death rituals, combined with Durkheim's work, they lay the groundwork for investigating African American culture through death rituals. It was the specific attention to African American death rituals that allowed A. D. Price, W. I. Johnson, and R. C. Scott to prosper. A reinterpretation or expansion of Durkheim's theory of rituals by Kertzer (1988) and Schwartz (1991) provides the bridge to investigating African American culture.

Barry Schwartz, in his article "Mourning and the Making of a Sacred Symbol: Durkheim and the Lincoln Assassination," addresses the conflict between the widespread negative perception of Lincoln before his assassination and the use of extraordinary funeral rites to elevate Lincoln to a sacred symbol. Until Kertzer's work in 1988, Durkheim's modern disciples assumed that society established sacred ideas, objects, or individuals by projecting onto them their positive communal values. In addition, society reserved its most majestic and imposing funeral rites for those individuals whom it most revered (Schwartz 1991, 344 and 360). Schwartz expands these ideas by showing how rituals can transform negative and controversial objects and individuals into positive figures. They become figures that embody only the community's most revered values. Thus, accepting Lincoln's transformation through death rituals from a controversial president to a sacred symbol provides a new way to understand Durkheim's theory of rituals.

Kertzer agrees with Durkheim that rituals bring a community together to share values and reinforce the group's culture, but Kertzer expands the role of rituals. He contends that rituals produce solidarity with or without shared values (Kertzer 1988, Schwartz 1991, 360). Rituals could be the catalysts to create common values out of conflicting community sentiments. Therefore, it is not always the society that co-opts the ritual to reinforce a society's common values, but the ritual itself can establish the solidarity and values for the community.

Kertzer's reinterpretation of Durkheim gave Schwartz the solution to Lincoln's transformation:

> Although people disagreed intensely about Lincoln's worth as president, their common participation in his funeral expressed and reinforced their common identification with the nation . . . It would be more precise to say that controversial objects, like the memory of Lincoln, promote solidarity only on the condition that they represent noncontroversial realities whose sacredness all recognize, ultimate realities on which a fundamental consensus rests. (Schwartz 1991, 360-361)

The funeral ritual has always been a social event meant to reinforce or maintain solidarity. People believed that they gathered to pay tribute to the individual, but their solidarity also reflected their devotion to societal values. Lincoln served as a surrogate for an intangible social aspiration, a collective hope that the country could pull together after a long, exhausting war. Lincoln's death unified the county's hopes to an extent that was virtually impossible for him to achieve during his life.

Schwartz's article on Lincoln identified three concepts that can provide insights into African American death rituals and thus African American culture. A ritual's ability to produce solidarity among various and conflicting values was the first cross-cultural concept. This explains why African American death rituals received acceptance from both races, different African tribes and the various status classes within the African American community. This universal acceptance created solidarity among African Americans despite conflicting sentiments in the community of mourners. Death rituals were the rare African American ritual that commanded this universality.

The second insight offered by Schwartz is the use of funeral rituals to transform and enhance the status of individuals. The hopes bestowed on Lincoln to heal a factious country were similar to the dreams of African Americans during the nineteenth and early twentieth century. The African American community transformed individuals upon death into symbols of freedom and, through the large funeral expenditures, economic prosperity. Despite the conflicting ideas about the social standing of African Americans in the United States, through death they became elite sacred symbols. In their desperate search for dignity, embracing death rituals was natural for African Americans because of the powers of transformation contained in death rituals. This search explains why the fraternal orders, which provided the social network in the African American community, usually offered death benefits. Through the fraternal network, nearly all community members could participate in the transformation process. It also explains why A. D. Price and R. C. Scott dedicated so much building space to the fraternal orders. If the fraternal orders provided a social outlet, dignity, and transformation into a sacred symbol, then it made good business sense for the funeral directors to play an integral part in these community events.

The last transferable point identified by Schwartz is American society's recognition that elaborate and well-orchestrated funerals were necessary for symbol making. The Union designed Lincoln's long multi-state funeral procession to enhance the creation of a state symbol. His casket slowly traveled by train from Washington to Springfield, Illinois. The trip included stops in most cities along the way for viewing. Crowds lined the railroad tracks even during the early morning hours when the train passed. In Chicago, over 80 percent of the city's residents observed or participated in the funeral procession (Schwartz 1991, 349). Communities competed to stage the most elaborate and dignified farewell. Lincoln was just one example of the state's expertise in staging elaborate funerals for the symbolism. John F. Kennedy's funeral is another example.

African American culture also recognizes that elaborate funerals create symbols. Together, the three insights Schwartz used to analyze Lincoln's funeral provide a historical and theoretical framework for this study. They connect death rituals in the African American community to the work of Durkheim and his followers.

Funeral rites and ceremonies are rites of passage. They create a transition from one state of existence to another for both the deceased and survivors (Rosenblatt, Walsh, and Jackson 1976, 7). However, this passage can occur only with a binding commitment by the group members to the roles, beliefs, status, and attitudes of the community. Whether it believes in an afterlife or not, the community must commit to a common understanding about death for this rite to take place. Theories dealing with commitment assert that commitments are greater when they are public instead of private, voluntary instead of involuntary, and involved instead of simple (Rosenblatt, Walsh, and Jackson 1976, 87-88). This school of thought demands public funerals in order for death to be meaningful for a society. Society does not recognize individual grieving and quiet burials because they fail to represent a commitment to that society. In contrast, a well-attended, public funeral publicly expresses a strong commitment on everyone's part.

The social aspects of funerals allow ethnic groups to preserve their sense of group solidarity despite society's larger transition from small intimate communities to larger, modern metropolises. This transition, due to industrialization and the rise of the city in the late nineteenth century, caused American society to question its values, work ethic, ideas of time, and gender roles. In contrast, Reconstruction, white Southern aggression, the association movement, and the great migration all served to strengthen African American cultural bonding in the years after the Civil War.

African American Funerals: An African Transplant

An African American self-consciousness emerged during the Harlem Renaissance in the 1920s. African Americans discovered that their culture and perspectives grew not only from the adoption and rejection of Euro-American characteristics, but also from the African world view. The African American relationship to American society was intricate and multifarious. Lawrence Levine discusses this pattern of simultaneous acculturation and revitalization in his book *Black Culture and Black Consciousness*. He states:

> Blacks shared with a number of other ethnic minorities a deep ambivalence concerning the degree to which they desired to enter the mainstream of white American culture because they shared with these other groups a strong centripetal urge which continually drew them back to central aspects of their traditions even as they were surging outward into the larger society. It was precisely because periods of increased opportunity and mobility posed the greatest threats to whole layers of black cultural tradition that such periods often witnessed important manifestations of cultural revitalization. (Levine 1977, 444-445)

The traditions that African Americans used for cultural revitalization were African, and funeral rituals had more direct connections to Africa than any other African American tradition. The community searched for ethnic identity in African culture and the African connections they found highlighted a very distinct African American idea of death. This study contends that the African American idea of death is an African transplant. Death beliefs are transplants that have not only nourished a successful profession in the African American community, as illustrated by the A. D. Price and R. C. Scott funeral homes, but are also responsible for the development of the two largest African American industries during the research period: banking and insurance.

At the turn of the century, leading scholars argued that the institution of slavery and pressure to assimilate American culture wiped out any remaining traces of African culture that survived the Atlantic voyage. In his book *The Myth of the Negro Past*, Melville Herskovits was the first major anthropologist to insist that African traditions had not only survived but had become part of American culture. Herskovits based his idea of

Africanisms on a belief of West African cultural homogeneity. Recent scholarship challenges Herskovits' West African assumptions, and traces the African source of African American culture to the Bantu culture of Central Africa (Vass 1979, Thompson 1983, Holloway 1990). Bantu dialects knitted a vast area of Central Africa into a common culture. Winifred Vass pioneered the theory of a Bantu origin for African American culture in her book *The Bantu Speaking Heritage of the United States*. Vass examined the African content in American language and culture and found their origin in the Bantu Central African culture (Holloway 1990, xii).

Understanding the specific African traditions that assimilated into American culture requires sensitivity to the tribal origins of New World Africans and the variety of customs inherent in these tribes. This analysis should use the dimensions of time and space to avoid being static. Ira Berlin argued in his article "Time, Space, and the Evolution of African American Society" that three distinct slave systems existed in America depending on place: a Northern nonplantation system and two Southern plantation systems, one around the Chesapeake Bay and the other in the Carolina and Georgia low country (Berlin 1986, 85). He further says that the development of African American culture and the social stratification in the culture depended on the ratio of recent African arrivals to second and third generation African Americans. This ratio depended on the period in the slave trade and the distinct slave system involved. This approach provides insight into the transformation of African death traditions to American.

The tremendous impact slavery had on economic and human development in the United States occurred despite the United States being only a marginal recipient of slaves exported from Africa. Philip Curtin in *The Atlantic Slave Trade: A Census* estimates that British North American imports made up only 4.2 percent of the entire Atlantic slave trade (Curtin 1969, 89) (Table 13 and Illustration 8). Because the small number of slaves imported into British North America arrived over a two hundred year period, the sporadic slave ships are easy to isolate. Using the port logs recorded by Elizabeth Donnan--the most precise and standard source for statistics on slave immigration to Virginia and South Carolina--origins of the 399,000 slaves imported to British North America become traceable (Herskovits 1941, 44; Curtin 1969, 143; Kulikoff 1977, 417).

Distribution of Slave Imports

Illustration 8

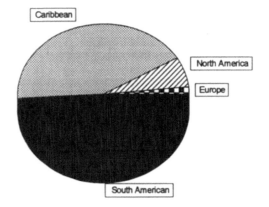

A Speculative Geographical Distribution of Slave Imports During the Whole Period of the Atlantic Slave Trade (000 Omitted) Table 13				
Region and Country	Total No.	No.	Total %	%
Grand Total	9,566		100.0	
Old World Traffic	175		1.8	
Europe		50		0.5
Madeira, Canaries,		25		0.3
Cape Verde Is.,				
Sao Thome'		100		1.0
North America	651		6.8	
Territory of the United	427		4.5	
States				
British North America		399		4.2
Louisiana		28		0.3
Middle America	224		2.3	
Mexico		200		2.1
Central America &		24		0.3
Belize				

A Speculative Geographical Distribution of Slave Imports During the Whole Period of the Atlantic Slave Trade (000 Omitted) Table 13			
Caribbean Islands	4,040		42.2	
Greater Antilles	2,421		25.3	
Haiti		864		9.0
Dominican Republic		30		0.3
Cuba		702		7.3
Puerto Rico		77		0.8
Jamaica		748		7.8
Lesser Antilles	1,619		16.9	
US Virgin Island		28		0.3
British Virgin Island		7		0.1
Leeward Island		346		3.6
Guadeloupe		291		3.0
Martinique		366		3.8
St. Vincent, St. Lucia, Tobago, & Dominica		70		0.7
Grenada		67		0.7
Trinidad		22		0.2
Barbados		387		4.0
Dutch Antilles		20		0.2
Bahamas		10		0.1
Bermuda		5		0.1

A Speculative Geographical Distribution of Slave Imports During the Whole Period of the Atlantic Slave Trade (000 Omitted) Table 13			
South America	4,700		49.1	
The Guianas	531		5.6	
Surinam & Guyana		480		5.0
French Guiana		51		0.5
Brazil	3,647		38.1	
Bahia		1,200		12.5
Other		2,447		25.6
Spanish South Ameriica	522		5.5	
Argentina, Uruguay, Paraguay, & Bolivia		100		1.0
Chile		6		0.1
Peru		95		1.0
Colombia, Panama, & Ecuador		200		2.1
Venezuela		121		1.3

Source: Philip D. Curtin. *The Atlantic Slave Trade: a Census*. Madison: University of Wisconsin Press, 1969. 88-89.

Documents Illustrative of the History of the Slave Trade to America, published by Elizabeth Donnan in 1935, includes manifest abstracts of slaving vessels that landed cargoes in ports of the continental United States. In the North before 1741, less than 30 percent of the slaves entering northern ports came directly from Africa due to a constant supply of white indentured servants (Berlin 1986, 90). While the North dramatically increased the number of imported African slaves for the next twenty years because of the European wars, after the wars the North switched back to European indentured servants and free laborers. Many aspects of African American culture in the Northern system had their origin during this twenty-year period. Unfortunately, the time dimension of the North's African acculturation is too short for large generalizations. Thus, this study concentrates on the two Southern plantation systems that provide critical masses of recent African arrivals over long periods.

Donnan's data came mainly from naval office records. The many gaps and incomplete portions of the list do not obfuscate several predominant patterns. Virginia and the Chesapeake region primarily imported slaves from the West Indies or nearby colonies before the 1680s (Kulikoff 1986, 320; Menard 1975, 34-35). As slavery expanded, both Southern plantation systems increased the percentage of slaves they imported directly from Africa except the South Carolina region. The South Carolina plantation system was the closest in style to the sugar colonies and had always imported slaves directly from Africa (Curtin 1969, 145). In the latter part of the eighteenth century, Virginia became a net supplier of slaves to the western territories from its own native population. South Carolina, which supplied much of the North Carolinian and Georgian market, continued to satisfy its own increasing needs in the eighteenth century by importing directly from Africa.

An important clue in learning a slave's probable origin is the date the merchant imported the African slave. When the researcher combines the slave's African origin with the type of American plantation system, the crops cultivated in that system, and the proportion of whites in the population, establishing the dynamics of African American community life is possible, including the probability for African customs to survive. For example, a slave in the Georgia plantation system confronted a high ratio of slaves to whites and a heavy importation of Africans. Thus, the Georgia system slave was better able to maintain African customs than a slave in the Northern plantation system, where African importation was sporadic and the ratio of slaves to whites was low (Kulikoff 1986, 318).

In the Chesapeake colonies between 1650 and 1690, most slaves were from the West Indies. They lived on small plantations of fewer than eleven African American slaves. By 1690, the slaves in the Chesapeake colonies made up only 15 percent of the population. The probability of African customs surviving during those years in that system is small. However, in the late 1680s the Chesapeake colonies expanded their direct African importation. The African proportion of the imported slave trade grew rapidly until, by 1740, more than nine-tenths of all slave immigrants were African and one-third of the slave population had left Africa or the West Indies within the previous ten years (Kulikoff 1986, 319-321). African slave imports into the Chesapeake colonies declined after 1740, but the proportion of African Americans in the population continued to rise and plantations increased in size. The African customs that existed in the 1730s were the ones most likely to affect early twentieth-century, African American life in the Chesapeake plantation area. By discovering the origins of the African slaves imported during this height of African exposure, one can identify the African customs with the best chance of survival.

The African supply network used by the British slavers was erratic at best. No region could maintain a steady and reliable supply of slaves. Yet when taken together, the slave exports did meet European demand. However, no individual coastal region exported slaves in a pattern similar to the rise and fall of New World demand. The origins of African slaves depended on the nationality of the port and the ships, colony preferences when there was a choice in the supply, and the period within which the importation took place. Based on a combination of these factors and Donnan's documents, Philip Curtin, in *The Atlantic Slave Trade*, derived projections of slaves imported into the North American mainland by origin.

Table 14 shows that the largest group of slaves imported into British North America was from Angola or West Central Africa (24.5 percent). In the eighteenth century, slavers commonly referred to Angola and West Central Africa as the Congo. Angolan slaves even dominated South Carolina (39.6 percent) because most of South Carolina's imports were late in the slavery period. Virginia imported 37.7 percent of its slaves from Bight of Biafra and only 15.7 percent from Angola between 1710 and 1769. However, Curtin's Virginia numbers raise several concerns. Curtin based his Virginia numbers on Donnan's Virginia sample. In this sample Donnan listed nearly half of the ships inbound from Africa as simply "from Africa" (Curtin 1969, 156). In addition, the period is too wide to identify the dominant group at the peak of African influence in Virginia. Allan Kulikoff addressed at least one concern in *Tobacco and Slaves* by looking specifically at slaves entering Yorktown, Virginia in 1718-1726 and 1728-1739. During the last great period of direct African influence between 1728-1739, Bight of Biafra remains the largest port of origin with 44 percent, but Angola is a close second with 41 percent. Unfortunately, this total sample of 8,786 still had many unknowns (34 percent). Yet, we can assume that the regions of Bight of Biafra and Angola both played significant roles in the African customs prevalent in the Chesapeake region during the 1740s.

Slaves Imported into the North American Mainland, by Origin Table 14				
Coastal Region of Origin	Per Cent of Slaves of Identifiable Origin Imported by			
	Virginia 1710-69	South Carolina 1733-1807	British Slave trade 1690-1807	Speculative Estimate, all Imported into North America (%)
Senegambia	14.9	19.5	5.5	13.3
Sierra Leone	5.3	6.8	4.3	5.5
Windward Coast	6.3	16.3	11.6	11.4
Gold Coast	16.0	13.3	18.4	15.9
Bight of Benin	---	1.6	11.3	4.3
Bight of Biafra	37.7	2.1	30.1	23.3
Angola	15.7	39.6	18.2	24.5
Mozambique-Madagascar	4.1	0.7	*	1.6
Unknown	---	---	0.6	0.2
Total	100.0	100.0	100.0	100.0

*Included in Angola figure.

Source: Philip D. Curtin. *The Atlantic Slave Trade: a Census.* Madison: University of Wisconsin Press, 1969. 157.

The South Carolina sample accurately shows that an overwhelming proportion of slaves entering the South Carolina and Georgia systems were from Angola (39.6 percent versus 19.5 from Senegambia). Despite the Yorktown, Virginia sample showing a higher percentage for Bight of Biafra versus Angola, most of the African slaves brought to the lower Southern system after 1740 came from the Portuguese ports in West Central Africa. One can debate which area in Africa dominated Virginia's African influence before the 1740s. However after the 1740s, it was the West Central African culture that dominated African influence in the South over the next sixty years. The dominant Central African culture during that period was Bantu.

> The Bantu of Central Africa possessed the largest homogeneous culture among the imported Africans and, consequently, had the strongest impact on the future development of African American culture and language. (Holloway 1990, xiii)

Therefore, one should concentrate on Bantu customs to investigate African transplants in African American death rituals.

THE BANTU CULTURE

During the early slaving days in the 1500s, the name "Kongo" was a specific reference to the Bakongo people. The "Kongo" region included modern Zaire and neighboring territories in modern Congo, Gabon, and northern Angola. As the slave trade in the region expanded exponentially and geographically, the term "Congo" was commonly used to label anyone who embarked from the West Coast of Central Africa. The name "Ngola" once referred to the ruler of the Ndongo part of the Kimbundu culture in what is now the northern part of modern Angola. The term "Angola" also became a common name for the whole west coast of Central Africa. This area stretched from Cape Lopez in Northwestern Gabon to Benguela on the coast of Angola proper (Thompson 1983, 103). Thus, by the eighteenth century, the terms "Congo," "Angola," and the West Coast of Central Africa were interchangeable.

The common use of the Bantu languages knitted these regions together. Many inhabitants of these regions spoke closely related, although not mutually intelligible, Bantu languages. The influence of the Bantu languages and culture spread over 2.5 million square kilometers during the centuries of European slave trading (Miller 1988, 8). The structural similarities, basic patterns, and grammatical matrix of the Bantu languages laid a foundation for many geographically dispersed people. Just as the many local variations of the Chinese language depend on the Chinese culture, the Bantu languages shared a common cultural background. Slaves from the West Coast of Central Africa shared fundamental beliefs and, despite being from different tribes, they could talk among themselves with some effort.

Plantation owners were very familiar with the agricultural practices and types of skills in various regions in Africa. A strong relationship existed between the type of agricultural cultivation and the imported African ethnic groups. Owners imported slaves from Central Africa primarily for field work. They had reputations as strong and vigorous workers (Holloway 1990, 14). Because most Southern owners isolated their field workers, the pressure to assimilate for the representatives of Bantu culture was less severe than for many other cultures. Their isolation allowed the Bantu to create a powerful sense of solidarity and retain a cultural foundation.

What was the makeup of the lands that formed West Central Africa? The following passage describes the region in terms of geography and hydrology:

> an elevated rolling surface, a thousand meters or more in altitude. Most of its rivers drained from a raised outer rim down into the vast, shallow depression of the central Zaire River basin, taking their sources along its wooded southern edge in the so-called southern savannas. The soils of the western parts of this savanna--roughly the plains drained by the Kasai River and its tributaries and by the streams flowing into the Lubilash and the Sankuru farther east--consisted of porous and infertile overlays of sands blown in over the ages from the Kalahari Desert to the south. The highest of these plains crested along an east-west watershed in the latitude of 10 degrees to 12 degrees south. To the south flowed the headwaters of the upper Zambezi . . . Thus, viewing the slaved regions of western central Africa as a whole, people tended to congregate in the wetter woodlands and forest-savanna mosaics of the inland plateaux between 4 degrees and 12 degrees south, with additional pockets of relatively concentrated population in the better-watered highlands and

river valleys and in the grassier areas around the middle
Zaire. (Miller 1988, 12, 13)

This geography limited the land that was useful for farming or raising
livestock.   Before European slaving operations, population growth
frequently expanded past support limits of the arable land, forcing many to
live in marginal sites.   Human mortality was extremely high.   Power
resulted from the ability to control the more desirable, productive land.
The powerless, forced to subsist in unfertile areas, frequently starved due
to droughts, or died of parasites and viruses.   Approximately once every
decade a perilous drought devastated the overexpanded population, creating
severe famine conditions and instigating outbreaks of epidemic disease.
Relocation only moved the powerless into more marginal living
environments.   These destabilizing events promoted a constant state of
tribal warfare and ideal conditions for European slave merchants.   Initially,
supplying Europeans with slaves allowed local leaders to dispatch their
enemies and secure more productive land with their new wealth and power.
The constant shifting of the slaving frontier promoted wars, conflicts, and
depopulation.   However, when the land ceased being the frontier and the
victorious trade kings resettled the land primarily with women and children
under their protection, a calm, productive, fertile, and prosperous period
followed (Miller 1988, 159).

The cost of maintaining power for this new generation of trading
kings was high.   Initially on the slaving frontier, the economic or political
cost of trading with the Europeans was small.   Raiding people on the
margins and locating ivory were by-products of their normal activities.   As
their economies demanded more European imports, the volume of slaves
necessary to maintain these new economies and the trading kings' power
became difficult to sustain.   An environment that traditional economics
would define as prosperous in terms of food, fertility, and peace became
a perilous situation when these traditional riches could no longer purchase
the rapidly appreciating European imports.   In a bid to preserve power,
many trading kings sacrificed even highly prized dependents to the slave
trade.

Depending on the geography of their homeland and their status
within their community, slaves exported to the New World brought some
agricultural or craft skills, but all brought similar fundamental beliefs.   The
slaves departing from the West Coast of Central Africa would be carrying
the following common cosmology:

The N'Kongo [i.e., an inhabitant of the capital of Kongo] thought of the earth as a mountain over a body of water which is the land of the dead, called Mpemba. In Mpemba the sun rises and sets just as it does in the land of the living . . ., the water is both a passage and a great barrier. The world, in Kongo thought, is like two mountains opposed at their bases and separated by the ocean.

At the rising and setting of the sun the living and the dead exchange day and night. The setting of the sun signifies man's death and its rising, his rebirth, or the continuity of his life. Bakongo believes and holds it true that man's life has no end, that it constitutes a cycle, and death are merely a transition in the process or change (Janzen and Macgaffrey 1974, 34; Thompson 1983, 106).

The Bakongo also believed in one God. This God gave the Bakongo strength through the spirits of their ancestors. The most effective medium for communicating with the ancestors was the grave (Nichols 1989, 13; Fenn 1989, 45; Thompson and Cornet 1981, 151). Inherent in this vision was an ancestral cult tied into the kinship system. Just as man's life did not end with death, man's power did not end with death. Power existed in Mpemba, the land of the dead, which was found below the water under the mountain of the living. Yet, more fundamental to the kinship system was the power directed through the water by ancestors to affect the living. Only elaborate funeral rites could secure a pledge of ancestral goodwill. Honoring the dead and practicing ostentatious funeral rituals were important survival techniques for the living.

The funeral was the true climax of life, and no belief drives deeper into the traditions of West African thought. For the problem of New World survivals this is of paramount importance, for whatever else has been lost of aboriginal custom, the attitudes toward the dead as manifested in meticulous rituals cast in the mold of West African patterns have survived (Herskovits 1941, 63).

The South, most notably South Carolina, produced many funeral customs that had direct parallel connections to Kongo beliefs. The placement of enchanted articles on graves, the uses of symbolic writings, and proper execution of funeral ritual were all major aspects of both African and

African American death customs used to protect the living and the dead. African American graves exist throughout the South with many dishes, shells, pipes, lamps, and clocks decorating their surface. Frequently these objects appear cracked, pierced with holes and/or turned upside-down. The people of the Kongo purposely splintered their grave decorations so the objects' spirits were free to join their former owner (Weeks 1914, 272; Fern 1989, 48) and inverted to symbolize the upside down world of the spirits (Thompson 1983, 142). In addition, by placing prized objects of the deceased on the grave, the Bakongo ensured that the deceased's spirit would not return to reclaim preferred or critical items (Glave 1891, 835; Fern 1989, 45).   Thompson documents in his book, *Flash of the Spirit*, scenes in Georgia during 1845-65, 1919, and 1939 where African Americans ritually placed the last object used by the deceased on the grave. "This was supposed to satisfy the spirit and keep it from following you back to the house" (Thompson 1983, 134). Kongo customs assert that the last strength of a dead person is still present within the last touched object. In the Kongo, one can touch the object and talk with the deceased through dreams and callings (Thompson and Cornet 1981, 200). When the object rests on the grave above the spirit, it can keep the spirit tied up and prevent the spirits from harming the living.

The Bakongo could look into the sun's dazzling reflection on the water and see the ancestral spirits. It was the brilliant flash that allowed them to see the spirits. They sought to recreate the flash in other shining objects. A unique feature of some African American graves is the use of broken glassware, silver paint, tin foil, bathroom tile, mirrors, and colored foil on potted plants to create the flash (Fern 1989, 48).

Seashells, symbols of the water that divides the land of life and death, and the chalky hue of the spirit world, held the soul's immortal presence and encompassed the spiraling cycle of life and death in the Kongo culture. Throughout the South, but especially in the Carolina low country, some graves made during the research period and for African American Vietnam war casualties had large seashells covering them (Thompson 1983, 135). Bakongo elders also planted trees on graves because the trees symbolized the spirit traveling to the world below. The spirit's travels could follow the roots of the tree. When my mother planted evergreens on both ends of my grandmother's grave, she never verbalized the symbolism, but knew it was something she wanted to do. These observations are not random examples but funeral rituals consistently practiced in the mid-twentieth century with direct ties to the African home of early slaves.

Circle dances in Africa became known as ring shouts or plantation walk-arounds in African American culture. Elaine Nichols who researched the religious and cultural significance of the circle dances in ceremonies, especially burials in West and Central Africa, describes a ring shout in the following manner:

> Although styles of shouts vary greatly from community to community, they share basic similarities. All ring shouts combine music and dancing in a counterclockwise circle. Shouters never cross their feet at the ankle. In some instances, the feet are never lifted from the floor, but are shuffled one in front of the other. While suitable for worldly dancing, African Americans believe that crossing the feet and lifting them from the floor are inappropriate for sacred dancing.
>
> Shouters clap their hands and move to the sounds of joyous songs or chants. While shouting, participants may become "possessed" with the holy spirit and enter a trance-like state. (Nichols 1989, 15)

Other African customs practiced in the New World by African Americans included passing children over the coffin of the deceased to protect them from spirits and fears of the dead. Families also placed randomly arranged writing on walls and in shoes to preoccupy evil spirits. Since evil spirits traveled in straight lines, the spirit became incapacitated if forced to decipher irregular patterns of symbols. All these precautions and rituals kept the spirit from returning to the land of the living and becoming a "plat-eyes"; a wandering evil spirit who could take a living or nonliving form and haunt and harm people (Nichols 1989, 16-17).

Besides African transplants in funeral customs, the predominance of secret societies and fraternal orders with death benefit features was another African transplant connected to death. Secret societies and the church were the two mainstays of African American communities. In 1870, Richmond's African American population of 46,220 men, women, and children supported more than 400 secret societies (Rachleff 1984, 25 and 203). The secret societies and fraternal orders provided the organizational structure for African Americans to help each other outside the auspices of church and kin. Herskovits asserts in his studies that most African permanent groupings, other than kinship units, possessed cooperative and even insurance features. The Dahomean had an aboriginal insurance system of mutual-aid societies that were permanent insurance societies. Their purpose was to assure proper performance at funerals. There was also a history in Africa of secret societies having religious bases or, occasionally, being actual cult groups (Herskovits 1941, 165-166).

African transplants in death and funeral rituals establish a cultural difference in African American death beliefs from other Euro-American ethnic beliefs. The reverence for ancestors promotes the importance of kinship and assures that the community pays proper attention to funeral rituals. I do not contend that the importance of death customs in African American culture is unique among American minority populations and ethnic groups. My point is that African transplants form the unique foundation that distinguishes African American beliefs and customs surrounding death.

Many American minorities face the problem of powerlessness in an American culture built on achievement and power. If death is the definitive symbol of human frailty, then a power-driven, achievement-based society would deny the reality of death. Joan Moore asserts that American and northern European cultures avoid acknowledging death because this denial is necessary to maintain faith in ones' ability to master the environment. How can the dominant society boast of controlling the physical, social, and psychological environment, if that society is powerless to influence the duration of its members' own stay on earth? Yet, for the discredited, underachieving, powerless groups, the human frailty that death represents is reality and death should take on a different meaning (Moore 1980, 73).

Richard Kalish, who has written and edited several books on death and ethnicity, uses the following quotation from Octavio Paz to describe how Mexican Americans (another discredited, allegedly underachieving and powerless group in America) view death:

> The word death is not pronounced in New York, in Paris, in London, because it burns the lips. The Mexican, in contrast, is familiar with death, jokes about it, caresses it, sleeps with it, celebrates it; it is one of his favorite toys and his most steadfast loves. True, there is perhaps as much fear in his attitude as in that of others, but at least death is not hidden away; he looks at it face to face, with impatience, disdain or irony. "If they are going to kill me tomorrow, let them kill me right away." (Paz 1961, 57-58; Kalish and Reynolds 1981, 158)

Among Mexicans and Mexican Americans there is even a Day of the Dead celebration where the dead receive candles, water, flowers, food, or incense.

> Thus, one can characterized the culture of Mexico by its interest in death. Mexico's interest in death strongly contrasts with denial and rejection in American culture. Yet, Mexican culture may also contain a pervasive anxiety about man's capacity to dominate and control his environment-- again, in sharp contrast with the United States. (Moore 1980, 75)

The theories of rituals outlined by Durkheim and Schwartz do not recognize the role of power, or specifically powerlessness, in creating solidarity within ethnic groups. Low levels of economic power can require community solidarity for economic survival along with cultural maintenance.

SUMMARY

Death rituals have had an important place in African American culture because of their universal acceptance in society, their ability to transform and enhance the status of individuals, and society's acceptance that elaborate funerals are necessary as symbolic statements. The African American community created a unique interpretation of these rituals based upon the assimilation of an African world view and the Euro-American perspective. The African influence, while adaptive to American practices, is still a dominant part of African American funerals today.

The information provided in this chapter is the "long foreground" that describes the cultural environment that A. D. Price found when he entered "the business." Later, R. C. Scott exploited this environment even further using technology and innovation. Together, they served the community by providing the symbolic statements that only well-capitalized, progressive firms could offer.

IV
Folk Beliefs and Current Practices

INTRODUCTION

Despite the powerless status of African American slaves, they could demand and receive one non-economic, culturally-based concession to their personal comfort: the right to bury their dead and conduct their own funeral services. Nearly all slave owners, whether reputed as cruel and inhuman or benevolent, honored this appeal, even though it typically allowed slaves from different plantations to gather on Sundays and during the night. In the rituals surrounding African American death customs, African American slaves found a decisive way to undermine the mythical foundations of the slave owners' world (Genovese 1974, 194). Given the dangers associated with African American slave death rituals, only strong cultural beliefs in both races explain the universal acceptance of these customs in the South.

AFRICAN AMERICAN SLAVE FUNERALS

Christopher Crocker researched death beliefs particular to the South in his article "The Southern Way of Death." Crocker's analysis revealed a "striking ideological characteristic of Southern funerals." This characteristic was an "explicit avoidance of moral or theological judgments" (Crocker 1971, 126) in Southern funerals. The absence of moral judgment entitled rapists, killers, gamblers, slaves, or other fringe elements of Southern society to the same comforts of a proper funeral as the morally correct Christian. Individuals cited God's judgment for the particular timing of a killer's or gambler's death, but the social commitment of the community was constant for all of the deceased. Because of this regional cultural belief, when African American slaves ardently insisted on proper funerals for their dead, Southern "moral" customs made it difficult for slave owners to ignore their pleas (Crocker 1971, 114-129; Genovese 1974, 194-202; Hatcher 1908, 36-37).

While granting the slaves' request for proper funerals, the slave owner did place restrictions on when and how the slaves conducted these rituals. Ironically, these restrictions allowed slave funerals to be closer to the slaves' African-based funeral customs. Most slave owners required burial to take place at night after completing the day's work. Later, they held the funeral services on a subsequent Sunday. The slaves probably preferred these "restricted" funeral arrangements. The torchlight funeral procession and the performance of rituals under the cover of darkness, perpetuated many African death customs, such as chants to the spirits and grave site dancing. Large gatherings of slaves from neighboring plantations were possible only at night and on Sundays. After the Civil War and into the late nineteenth-century, this practice survived and most African American funerals continued at night and on Sundays.

Cultural acceptance of African American funeral practices did not imply that whites were comfortable with the practical implication of their moral concessions. They confronted their worst fears in 1800 when Gabriel Prosser organized an insurrectionist plot during a child's funeral congregation (Genovese 1974, 194). After preacher Nat Turners' revolt in 1831, Virginia passed a law to ban sermons from African American preachers and public funerals without a white official present. The law however, did not diminish the role or importance of slave funerals. In practice, despite the potential problems with slave funerals, most slave owners encouraged or at least tolerated them. Even slave owners who did not have moral or religious convictions against banning slave funerals felt that allowing African American funeral rites reduced the potential for violent slave rebellion. Obviously, the slave owners had a greater fear from banning funeral rites than the potential disruptions from the gatherings.

Acquiescence to slave funeral customs did not mean slave owners refrained from taking advantage of the slaves' reverence for the grave. In Barbados, where African Caribbeans could testify in legal proceedings involving themselves or freedmen, non-baptized slaves swore an oath on grave dirt, instead of the Bible (Handler and Lange 1978, 207-208). One planter remarked:

> the solemnity of that oath ["by grave dirt"] appears to be connected with their ideas of the survivance of departed souls, and of future rewards and punishments under the decrees of the Divine Power. (Steele 1787-88, in Handler 1978, 208)

Respect for the power and significance of death rituals did not keep African Americans or whites from exploiting these customs to provoke specific reactions from each other.

The general cultural acceptance of African American funeral

customs served to establish two foundations for the African American community. Funerals provided a mechanism for constructing social organizations, and established the role and relevance of the African American preacher. While the African American funeral in the antebellum period was a white-sanctioned religious ritual, the funeral as a social event, cultural builder, and pageant may be the more significant aspect of this antebellum American ceremony. The opportunity to come together, conduct a ritual according to their own ideas, and share this experience with an extended group of their peers made this occurrence a unique and significant event for African Americans during slavery. Funerals gave slaves an opportunity to establish a cultural identity. They instilled personal values beyond the reach of slave owners. Within their strictly dominated environment, death customs offered the slaves one realm where they controlled their fate.

African American social organizations have a long history of using death customs as a foundation and legitimizing cover. In 1790, a group of free, light-skinned African Americans in the city of Charleston successfully banded together and met as a funeral society under the name Brown Fellowship Society. The Society ensured decent funerals by buying land in 1794 on Pitts Street. The land became their personal cemetery. Later, they found it convenient and acceptable to the white ruling elite to construct a society hall on the same plot. Darker-skinned, free African Americans formed another funeral society named the Humane Brotherhood and followed a similar pattern by buying a burial lot next to the Brown Fellowship lot. A fence separated each society's plot (Clarke 1979, 136). Both groups were extremely conservative, very status conscious, and considered "good citizens" by the authorities. Significantly, the desire for proper funerals provided the vehicle for these early African American social organizations. Therefore, death customs provided an important foundation for the construction of an autonomous African American community.

The other major outcome of the African American community's funeral customs was the preeminent status of the preacher. Slaves insisted on having an African American "preach the funeral" even after the ban on African Americans preaching without a white official present. Because the speaker preached the Sunday funeral sermon to a large gathering of slaves from many plantations and without the imposition of many white-church restrictions, only the best African American orators and preachers received speaking invitations. The presence of a well-known African American preacher showed the status of the deceased and the slave owner. For the slave owners, having renowned African American preachers come to their plantation reflected on the slave owner's social prestige.

> An [African American] funeral without an uproar,
> without shouts and groans, without fainting women and
> shouting men, without pictures of triumphant deathbeds and
> the judgment day, and without the gates of heaven wide open
> and the subjects of the funeral dressed in white and rejoicing
> around the throne of the Lamb, was no funeral at all.
> (Hatcher 1908, 38)

The fiery and thrilling oratory style developed during funeral sermons became institutionalized in African American churches once they broke away from the existing religious orders.

By the early nineteenth century, many African Americans observed and accepted the basic tenets of European Christianity. Most African Americans flocked to the Methodist and Baptist churches (Fauset 1944, 4-8; Frazier 1939, 31; Park 1919; 118-19). However, coexistence with whites within the established churches was problematic and fueled the desire to form separate churches:

> The chief reasons for these separatist tendencies were the
> reluctance of white Christians to accept [African Americans]
> in the already established churches on a plane of equality,
> and the desire of [African Americans] to worship in churches
> where they could feel free to express themselves along the
> lines which the general condition of their lives prompted.
> (Fauset 1944, 8)

By 1825, the African Methodist Episcopal, the African Methodist Episcopal Zion, and the Negro Baptist church had all become established denominations for African Americans (Fauset 1944, 6).

African Americans expressed the general conditions of their lives through their death customs. An emotional and spectacular commemoration of death served as a form of communal catharsis in African American culture. During the ceremony, participants ecstatically appealed to spirits of the present and past. It was the preacher's role to incite the mourners' emotions and achieve this catharsis. Night funerals with torches, grave site dancing, and fires were vital elements in the drama and pageantry (Sobel 1988, 200):

> In 1835 a "Taxable Citizen of Ward Four" wrote to the
> Southern Patriot of Charleston: There are sometimes every
> evening in the week funerals of negroes accompanied by
> three or four hundred negroes and a tumultuous crowd of
> other slaves who disturb all the other inhabitants in the
> neighborhood of burying grounds . . . Such is frequently the
> crowd and noise made by them that carriages cannot safely
> be driven that way. (Epstein 1977, 235)

This white citizen's remark illustrates the tensions between whites and
African Americans and the cultural gap in their conceptions of properly
exhibited emotion. African American preachers understood this special
need of their community from the beginning. Talented preachers emerged
and many Christian burial societies organized themselves around a
successful preacher whose ability could assure proper veneration and
pageantry for African American dead.

    Prayer was the medium of communication between the preachers
and their congregations. African American prayers portrayed life as a
journey, a journey that did not take health or life for granted. Most
prayers expressed sincere humility for the right to exist, and an
appreciation for abrupt and quick contact with death and illness (Folly
1980, 5-6). The African American preacher reached his congregation
through an emotional appeal to basic beliefs: friendship, duty, honor, fear,
shame, emulation, patriotism, compassion, etc.

> The minister, even when not striking directly at fear-
> producing descriptions of death, likes to talk about things
> with which death has some connection. Any mention of the
> grave or of death serves the purpose--to produce shouting.
> Jesus' triumph over the great mystery, death, is most
> effective: "When Bold Almighty's Son got ready to come
> out of the grave, He busted the grave and blinded dem men
> and put 'em to death, God bless yo' souls, and come on
> out."(Pipes 1951, 112-113)

Invoking the fear of God, commonly translated into the fear of death (Pipes
1951, 110-112), was a primary technique for generating emotion.

    A tremendous challenge for the minister was preaching the funeral
of a fringe member of the community. The ability of ministers to elicit
emotion from the congregation was a real test of their skill and knowledge.

Cultural norms demanded that the individual receive a proper burial without moral or religious judgment. Illustrated in chapter six is an account of this type of funeral sermon. In this example, the deceased was a nonreligious, successful businessperson whom the community strongly disliked. While the preacher's success is questionable, his devotion to the principle of all people receiving a proper service and his relationship to his congregation is readily apparent.

Analyzing funerals and funeral ministers reveals African American attitudes at the time of death. However, to add information on the everyday perspective toward death and death rituals, the researcher must also rely on folk expressions. The next section reviews African American music as a way to uncover attitudes about death in the common African American experience.

SONGS

The songs composed and sung by African Americans best illustrate written attitudes and expectations about death. Analyzing the two primary forms of African American music, spirituals and blues, offers insight into African Americans' relationship with life and death. These forms also illustrate how African Americans ritualized this relation and wove it into their folk customs.

In the early twentieth century, intellectuals debated the origin of African American spirituals. In one camp, Newman White (White 1928) and George Jackson (Jackson 1933) refuted the notion that African American spirituals sprung from African origins. Opposing that interpretation was Melville Herskovits (Herskovits 1941), discussed in the first section, and Sterling Brown (Brown 1958 & 1969). They argued that the differences between African American music and other American music styles were so great that one must acknowledge the African influence. No matter the origin, the treatment of death in African American spirituals uniquely bonds these spirituals to the African American experience. They express death as a symbol of liberation that does not have a counterpart in white culture. W. E. B. Du Bois' essay "Of the Sorrow Songs" in *The Souls of Black Folk* takes a very enlightening and interpretive look at these spirituals. He called them "sorrow songs" because they were "the music of an unhappy people, of the children of disappointment; they tell of death and suffering and unvoiced longing toward a truer world, of misty wanderings and hidden ways" (Du Bois 1990, 182). Yet the songs never gave up hope and were always optimistic about life. The dichotomy between optimism and gloom and embracing, yet fearing, death was a collective confirmation of Du Bois' dualities. African Americans had to present an acceptable image in public, while reserving their true feelings for private moments. This was not a veil that whites had to wear.

John Lovell in his book *Black Song* points out that finding an obtrusive horror of death in African American spirituals is rare. Though acknowledging its ultimate power, the spirituals portray respect for and almost a benevolent relationship with death.

> After all, Death is only doing what he has to. He realizes that if he let you know far in advance, you would only build a grand case of nerves. In the spiritual, Death hardly ever pounces and drags you away, screaming.
>
> The fact that death is associated with rewards and deliverance softens his image considerably. The fact that Death is an undercurrent symbol for the road to freedom on earth makes him, many times, a positively welcome figure. (Lovell 1972, 306)

Death as a symbol of freedom, allows one to move beyond interpreting these songs as simply religious expressions of a spiritual life. Death as a symbol of freedom underscores the contrast between uplifting spirituals and the realities of slave existence. The songs judged by the plantation owners as safe because they referred to the afterlife for salvation, were in reality rebellious expressions pointing to the North and freedom. During this period, religion had a social and political role similar to funerals. The African American spirituals express the desire for freedom and justice by judging ones' betrayers. They illustrate a tactical battle in which the proper strategy or attitude would gain the believer an everlasting future (Cone 1972, 14-15; Lovell 1969, 134-136). The aspirations expressed in the spirituals--freedom, justice for the slaves, and reward for righteous living--were only available through the final rite of passage, death.

James H. Cone, in his book *The Spirituals and the Blues*, describes the blues as secular spirituals. They parallel spirituals because they conduct the same search for truth in the African American experience. However, the blues are secular because they restrict their examination of the African American experience to the "immediate and affirm the bodily expression of black soul, including its sexual manifestations" (Cone 1972, 112). Spirituals revealed the aspirations and goals of the antebellum

African American experience. The blues expressed the burden of African American experiences after the Civil War, battered between the gains from emancipation and the economic realities of segregation. In contrast to the communal and collective voices spoken through spirituals, the voice of the blues was personal and individualistic. The blues attempted to make people aware of common individual problems suffered by African Americans in their struggle to exist amid constant degradation and denial. The blues became the voice of the African American proletariat; its message was suffering, the burden of freedom, and the precarious existence of African Americans in post-Civil War America. Blues emerged into a lifestyle and identity for the African American community (Cone 1972, 123).

While the spirituals offer symbolism and imagination to escape from reality, the blues confronted the everyday aches and pains of life. Whether hell existed was irrelevant if your man had left, the law wanted you, or you had lost your job. A strict moral doctrine within the church forced some people to seek another outlet for everyday life.

> [The blues] emphasize the experiences of this life, of the here and now, and flaunt the celebration of a deep sense of sensuality. Sensuality here is used in the broadest, most fundamental sense. The poetry and aesthetic of blues celebrate touch, tastes, smells, sights, and sounds of this life. (Folly 1976, 55)

Many African Americans felt they had to choose between behaving meekly as the church instructed, which earned their reward in the next life, or living for today in the lifestyle represented by the blues. The contradictions between the biblical promised land and the everyday suffering African Americans experienced became a form of the blues itself. However, the popularity of the blues was not a rejection of God in the eyes of the blues singer, but an acknowledgment of life's rocky road.

The tension between the minister and the bad street-corner man is a favorite theme in folk tales. The blues and folk tales ridicule the preacher for allegedly using the promise of a joyous afterlife to secure real advantages from his primarily female congregation. In his book *Positively Black*, Roger D. Abrahams collected several folk tales commenting on the preacher's hypocrisy. He discussed the tension:

To understand why these stories have remained such a vital part of the repertoire of the jokester one must remember that the streetcorner man-of-words has a real rival for word power and status in the preacher. The street-man, whether he subscribes to cat or hardman values, is classified as a sinner, and as such is focused upon by the preacher in his sermons. There is a natural assumption by the street-man that this occurs only as a way of garnering power, especially over the women in the congregation, thus being able to exploit them in terms of food, sex, and money. Since this is accepted as a norm (if not an ideal) for interpersonal activity, it is not the exploitation to which the street-man objects, but rather the rivalry that has proved in the long run, to be out of balance. In contests for allegiances and exploitability, the preacher always seems to win, thus the attribution of hypocrisy and charlatanism. And what makes the defeat all the more bitter is that the preacher is attracted to the same kind of life style as the street-man, with the Cadillacs, the beautiful clothing, and the retreat in the Bahamas surrounded by beautiful women. (Abrahams 1970, 105-106)

Although consistently losing to the preacher, the blues singer has only one request, reflecting the absolute recognition of how little one should expect from life:

Well, there's one kind favor I ask of you,
One kind favor I ask of you,
Lord, there's one kind favor I ask of you,
Please see that my grave is kept clean. (Cone 1972, 142)

Death in the blues was immediate and final. The blues did not presume an afterlife or a reward for today's behavior. No one promised a future so the songs advocated enjoying the few pleasures of today. Denial of a future life encouraged individuals to concentrate on the pleasure and sensuality of their current life (Folly 1980, 54-72). Consistent with this 'here and now' philosophy, the blues celebrated death with large funerals and feasting--events with tangible benefits that one's peers could enjoy. After the body was lowered into the ground, the blues no longer recognize the soul's existence. The blues fostered a very immediate and emotional treatment of death.

These secular and sacred songs give us two ways to look at death and consequently two ways to interpret the African American experience. The sacred perspective views death as the beginning, an entrance to the spiritual world. It requires one to focus on this world only to receive rewards in the next world. The sacred view assumes that African Americans were not comfortable with this world or death as a phenomenon of this world (Jackson 1972, 204).

The secular perspective pronounces death a common and inevitable event that is part of the natural process. Given the exceedingly high African American mortality rate from disease, war, crime, and lynching in the late nineteenth century, death was a very frequent companion for African Americans. It was unavoidable and final. From the secular perspective, the joys and sorrows of life could only come from a meager set of everyday experiences (Jackson 1972, 204).

The sacred approach to death established the reverence and cultural dominance that funerals enjoy in African American culture. However, secular pragmatism bestows on funeral practices their centrality. Because death is the final point for the living, it is the last, and often only, opportunity to establish one's social status and meaning for being on this earth. The combination of sacred reverence, secular pragmatism, and status opportunities created substantial opportunities for shrewd entrepreneurs such as A. D. Price and R. C. Scott. Custom dictates a proper funeral and audience. This happens without regard to the deceased's moral choices during life. During the research period, money was available for funerals in unusually large amounts. Often, this was the first time a family had access to a large sum of money to make a status statement. Because most of the society judged funerals a safe and acceptable form of expression, there were few constraints on the rituals from outside the African American community. Thus, many people attempted to achieve lifetime goals of power, respect, and status through funerals and death customs. In Richmond, the community put their faith in R. C. Scott and his colleagues as the skilled masters of transformation and the providers of lifetime dreams.

Social control within the African American community was an outgrowth of the sacred doctrine. A person lived a socially responsible life because death would occur and the fate of the soul depended on past actions. Concern for the fate of the soul was one of a community's strongest weapons to insure conformity to cultural norms. "You preach your funeral while you living, your eulogy is just a reminiscence of your life" (Folly 1980, 17). Yet, relying on the fear of death to maintain social control, in reality, was an empty threat. Crocker has pointed out that death customs, at least in the South, were indistinguishable between nonsinners and sinners. In fact,

> books of instruction for funerals written by Southern ministers for their regional colleagues insist that the most morally reprehensible of persons should be pictured during the burial service as enjoying the fruits of salvation. This is deemed a proper and fitting response not so much for the immediate family's sake, but in terms of doctrine and faith. (Crocker 1971, 126-127)

Thus, the minister's actions reward the secular approach to life by removing a religious denial of proper burials.

The tension between the sacred and secular was a signature characteristic of the African American church. Besides the spiritual instruction of their congregation, African American churches and ministers engaged in political activism in public forums (Childs 1980, 1). However, churches and ministers usually limited their political activism to the concerns of the local congregation.

African American ministers were not the only leaders with political power in the community. Respect within the African American community and organizational proficiency did not ensure wide-scale political power for African American leaders. Instead, the acceptance and approval of the white establishment conferred political power. For example, Booker T. Washington wielded national political power with the help of strong ties to the white establishment, in contrast to W.E.B. Du Bois or Marcus Garvey, who had strong African American support, but few white backers. While some ministers were among the approved civic leaders, other professions were more vital and economically important to the local white business people and political powers.

> Traditionally, Negro civic leaders occupying symbolic positions of respect were "tapped" by leaders in the white community as contact points. The influence of such "anointed" figures often depended more on their near monopoly over liaison channels to the all important white communities' decision-makers than on any spontaneous following within the Negro community which they might have generated. Undertakers, insurance men, bankers,

teachers, a few professional men Above all, ministers of
Negro churches; these were the men who traditionally were
treated as spokesmen for their local Negro communities.
Accommodationist, conservative, dignified, personally
successful men: they have been for more than half a century
the prime models for Negro children asking to be shown
local "men of influence."(Marvick 1965, 123)

Among the occupations identified above, only the undertaker or funeral
director combined religion, financial resources, and a cultural mandate.
They possessed the traits necessary for access to powerful elite circles.
This access allowed them to wield tremendous power and establish
themselves as power brokers. R. C. Scott's close relationship with Judge
Gunn persuaded the court to establish the Virginia Mutual Life Insurance
Company out of the National Benefit Life Insurance Company's bankrupt
assets. This one act of power brokering created a company that *Black
Enterprise* ranked eighteenth among African American Insurance
Companies in 1987. As of December 31, 1987, the company had $4.259
billion of assets and $12.862 billion of insurance in force (Butler 1991,
307-308).

CULTURAL ROLE OF AFRICAN AMERICAN FUNERAL DIRECTORS

The key to the central role of African American funeral directors in
the community is their important connection to African American social
organizations. Nearly all African American organizations before the Civil
War and a majority after the war, until the turn of the century, stated that
their purpose was to furnish sickness and death benefits. A pauper burial
is among the deepest horrors of the human experience. Humans regard
virtually no other act with such shame and loathing (Hoffman 1919, 22).
Crocker illustrates this by stating "one of the most damning moral
classifications a Southerner can apply is, 'He's so mean he didn't or
wouldn't go to his own mother's funeral'" (Crocker 1971, 124). Folk
literature supports this idea in critical scenes where, despite the dangers,
the folk hero-criminal respectfully attends a relative's funeral in disguise.
As sickness and burial associations developed more sound business
practices, they laid the foundation for other organizations--religious
denominations, the insurance industry, and banking--and they provided
tremendous pools of accumulated capital. In a period when there were few

large-scale, African American businesses, the three largest--banking, insurance and the church--depended on the services and financial support of the funeral industry for their survival. With this support, each of these enterprises became indispensably instrumental in the economic progress of the African American community.

The first known sickness and burial organization, the "Free African Society" started in Philadelphia in 1778. Richard Allen, who founded the African Methodist Episcopal Church, and Absalom Jones, a distinguished African American preacher in the Episcopal Church, started the society. The Free African Society had L42 9s 1d on deposit in the Bank of North America in 1790 (Browning 1937, 417). Du Bois in his study of African Americans in Philadelphia made the following observation about sickness and burial organizations in that city:

> By 1838 there were 100 such small groups, with 7,448 members, in the city. They paid in $18,851, gave $14,171 in benefits, and had $10,023 on hand. Ten years later about 8,000 members belonged to 106 such societies. Seventy-six of these had a total membership of 5,187. They contributed usually 25 cents to 37 1/2 cents a month; the sick received $1.50 to $3.00 a week and death benefits of $10.00 to $20.00 were allowed. The income of these 76 societies was $16,814.23; 681 families were assisted. (Du Bois 1899, 222)

In the city of Charleston, the city authorities viewed the Brown Fellowship Society and the Humane Brotherhood with a complacent and satisfied eye (Clarke 1979, 136). Nevertheless, in 1815 the societies rebelled. Whites in the city decided to build a hearse house on the land these organizations had set aside for burials. In protest, the societies quickly orchestrated the removal of 4,367 African American church members from Charleston Methodist churches and formed the African Methodist Episcopal Church of Charleston under the ministry of Morris Brown. Unfortunately, the Charleston branch of the church existed for only a short time. By 1820, the legislature had revoked their right to worship and had torn the church down. When white citizens discovered an insurrectionist plot by Denmark Vesey in 1822, who was still a member of the African Methodist Episcopal Church of Charleston, it brought an end to the church (Clarke 1979, 125-127). Yet, the catalyst for starting the original church and political action against Charleston was the attack on African American sacred grounds.

Although important before the Civil War, the significance of sickness and burial societies to free African Americans increased drastically after the Civil War when the ranks of potential free members soared. In Richmond, for example, nearly all religious, work, and community activities flowed through a network of these organizations.

> With limited resources and in an atmosphere of continual social conflict, Richmond African Americans built an impressive community. They wove together the formerly free and the formerly slave, the city native and the "country negro," dark-skinned and light-skinned, literate and illiterate, skilled and unskilled. The initial building block was the extended family, a resilient, vital social institution. Linked with it was the church. Together, they nourished a common set of relationships. Built on this foundation, a broad network of social organizations called "secret societies" fulfilled a multiplicity of purposes: funerals and death benefits, trade organization, collective self-education and self-improvement, religious advancement, political expression, socializing, and the like. Woven together, and interwoven with extended families and church organizations, these secret societies were the circulatory system of the black community. (Rachleff 1984, 13)

By the 1870s, Richmond could boast of more than 400 different secret societies overseeing the social interaction of the community (Rachleff 1984, 25). In Washington, on March 24, 1862, the *National Republican* commented that:

> there has never been a colored person buried in Washington at the public expense. The people of color in the District have charitable societies among themselves--numbering some thirty in all--which take care of the sick and bury the dead. Neither the public nor the government has ever been called on for a farthing for these objects. (Borchert 1980, 139)

People joined these organizations because they provided support in times of need. They gave people without identities an identity. They bestowed status, insured payment to the funeral director, and guaranteed a proper burial.

The popularity of burial associations produced many benefits for the

African American funeral director. Since the associations set the guidelines for their members, the funeral director could concentrate on the technical aspects of the funeral. In addition, the association relieved the funeral director from making assessments and negotiating payments because each person joined an association that fit his or her financial and social status needs. As insurance companies replaced the sick and burial societies, they solved the problem of guaranteed payments, but were unable to address the other two features of the societies. Insurance companies provided more stable finances, but there were no assurances that the purchased funeral would meet the individual's social status needs. Mrs. Alice Wine, a longtime resident of Johns Island, South Carolina, discussed this tradeoff in Guy and Candie Carawan's book *Ain't You Got a Right to the Tree of Life?*

> Society is better than insurance to me. That society is supposed to tend the sick and bury the dead. Everybody who in there pay dues. They write from twenty-five cents up to one dollar a month. You is a twenty-five-cent member, you get twenty-five dollars when you die; you is a fifty-cent member, you get fifty dollars; you is a seventy-five-cent member, you get seventy-five dollars; you is a dollar member, you get a hundred dollars. Just as much as you pay, that's as much you get out. If you be sick, society service two person out to sit down with you all night, every night, until you get better or worse. If you don't go and sit, you be have to pay a dollar fine. If you sick and aren't able to pay your bills, they keep it up for you, live or dead; they elect money from the table and they keep you arrear. Insurance not going to do that.
>
> And then the insurance man going to give you your money-put it on the table. Now, how you going to bury? That money can't move to dig grave. But that society there, they treat you all right. They don't give you your money and leave you there. They give you your money and give you attention. And we got pallbearers and everything in there. We got the pallbearers to take you from the undertaker and bring you to the church; take you from the church and carry you in the graveyard. They put you down there, and we got the member to cover you up. See, that's done. (Carawan 1989, 75)

As the insurance industry slowly replaced the sickness and burial societies at the end of the nineteenth century, the funeral directors raised their profile and services to provide the social needs alluded to by Mrs. Alice Wine. The societies allowed individuals to preplan and insure a proper funeral according to each member's definition. With few guidelines on funeral etiquette, limited pre-funeral planning with the deceased, and family status on the line, families began surrendering all decisions to professional funeral directors. The professional relieved the families and took care of all the details for an appropriate price.

Another source of funeral directors' authority in the African American community during the late nineteenth and early twentieth centuries was their unique ability among the African American merchants to demand and receive cash instead of credit. The inability of African American small business owners to grant credit drove many out of business. A shortage of money forced patrons to bypass African American-owned stores and shop where there was sufficient credit available. Funeral directors not only had most of their bills paid in cash or goods up-front, but received compensation for high ticketed items and service. Among merchants and professionals, including doctors and lawyers, the funeral director was the rare merchant whose stature and type of service made up-front payment an unquestioned canon of the community.

The client visiting a funeral establishment to arrange and purchase services had to do so under tremendous time constraints. Frequently, the funeral director had the body before the family and funeral director had a conference to decide the arrangements. Because removing the deceased from the original funeral home for any reason was highly unusual for survivors, especially an inability to agree on a price, time worked to erode any client's resistance to professional suggestions. The lack of time and cultural correctness precluded price shopping among different funeral homes. The short period between the arrival of the deceased and the burial, forced the funeral director to establish predictable patterns. These patterns assured the performance of a culturally acceptable funeral service efficiently delivered with no surprises. The funeral director entered the negotiations with an incentive to emphasize services selected from a fixed and familiar inventory of arrangements. Since the preparation of the body usually began before the family started negotiating with the funeral director, the families were effectively limited to that establishment's inventory of services.

Families subconsciously reinforced a culturally-based inventory of services when they chose an ethnic funeral director. In 1977, the Federal Trade Commission investigated the history and practices of the funeral industry. The FTC concluded that while the choice of a funeral director might reflect social class, status, and geographic convenience, the choice was generally ethnically-oriented (Federal Trade Commission 1977, 18). This selection process consistently established the funeral director as a prime cultural leader and purveyor of the African American community identity.

Families became tremendously dependent upon the funeral director to lead them through the process. The average person has to arrange a funeral once every fifteen years (Mitford 1963, 28). Thus, most family negotiators had no familiarity with relative prices, procedures, the services needed, or protocol. They entered the funeral home with few facts and virtually no knowledge of legal requirements and prohibitions (Federal Trade Commission 1977, 29). For example, although funeral directors routinely embalmed the body upon arrival and before the family conference, no state laws required embalming except for interstate travel by common carrier. The only exception to this routine was among orthodox Jews (Gebhart 1928, 19). Ignorant of proper procedures and overcome with emotions, the family entrusted the funeral director with the family's status, community image, and respectful homage to the deceased. Usually the funeral director deserved this blind trust, but the client was vulnerable:

> While it is not uncommon for whites to surrender valuable [insurance] policies to morticians, the black's ignorance about the workings of . . . insurance language, burial precedents, union benefits and his probability of not having read the insurance contract, all combine to make him exceptionally vulnerable to exploitation. When the director indicates he will take care of everything he often does just that. (McDonald 1973, 144)

Why does ethnicity establish the primary selection criteria for choosing a funeral home? As late as the 1960s, when Christopher Crocker conducted his interviews on death customs among middle and upper-lower class whites in two communities in North Carolina, he found that:

white informants corroborated accounts in the existing
literature that a "proper funeral" is defined partly in
opposition to the supposed characteristics of [African
American] funerals. (Crocker 1971, 115)

These ethnic characteristics divide into two primary headings. First, the
use of funeral rites as a form of celebration and second, the high degree of
emotion exhibited during the rituals.

In the study period, the intensified family unity during bereavement
turned the funeral into a celebration (McGee and Scoby 1981, 1). The
African American funeral was not only able to alleviate geographic
isolation for the extended family, but bridge emotional divisions. An
accurate description of this social event would be the ratification of the
family's strength through the celebration of death. The organization and
preparation for the impromptu family reunion forced large segments of the
family to become active participants and brought them into the circle of the
bereaved. The successful staging of the funeral feast was an expected
event (McGee and Scoby 1981, 48; Lunceford and Lunceford 1976, 36)
and an integral part of reaffirming the family's identity. The funeral rituals
in the twentieth century served the same purposes that they had during
slavery. These rituals preserved the family structure against the effects of
cultural disintegration and economic pressure. It was a survival technique.

Even family members and friends on the fringe of the community
could show their respect and bond with the family by serving as grave
diggers. Grave diggers were peripheral participants and custom excused
them from attending the funeral rites at the church, where their presence
might be unsettling. The grave digger's work clothes allegedly excused
them, although one suspects that the typical liberal indulgence in liquor
during the digging was a factor (Hill 1976, 177). Regardless, grave
diggers did attend the funeral feast.

African Americans were not alone among ethnic groups in
conducting funeral feasts. However, there was more emphasis on the feast
as an integral part of African American death customs and it was a defining
characteristic of African American funeral rites by the whites interviewed
by Crocker.

Charlotte L. McGee and Phyllis Scoby conducted a set of interviews
with African American and white funeral directors in Los Angeles during
the 1970s. In these interviews, both sets of directors still agreed that the
major difference between the actual funerals of African Americans and
whites was the "overt and uninhibited display of emotionalism" exhibited

at African American funerals (McGee and Scoby 1981, 57). It was the African American funeral directors' understanding and attention to this emotionalism that established their claim of more desirable service for their clients.

The "female attendant" is an example of ethnic adaptation for the sake of emotionalism. The literature suggests no services of this type at any white funeral homes. She was the center of the consolation effort provided by African American funeral home for the bereaved. Although she could offer comfort to both men and women, widows primarily received her attention.

> A female chauffeur was provided whenever a woman lost her husband. This female chauffeur, dressed in black, remained with the widow during the service. She escorted her outside, brought her to the limousine, chauffeured her to the cemetery, and sat down with her at the interment service. This woman, usually, checked on the widow a few times during the week following the funeral service. (Masamba and Kalish 1976, 31)

It is debatable whether funeral directors responded to emotional needs or whether they shared in the creation of emotionalism. The funeral preacher strived to create emotion among the mourners. The preacher's greatest fear at the Funeral of Brother Jesse Harding was the congregation not generating enough emotion (Chapter 6). The songs became an integral part of funeral services because of their ability to generate emotion. Finally, the African American preacher and funeral director used visual confrontations of death to achieve emotional catharsis. Examples of visual confrontations of death were pictures of the deceased on the funeral service bulletin or closing an open casket during the service (Masamba and Kalish 1976, 31-33). When engaging in this spiritually cleansing process, it was vital and prudent to possess services such as the female attendant and tie these services to an ethnic base.

SUMMARY

I do not assert that African American funeral directors consciously viewed their job as holding the scepter of African American heritage or fleecing their clients of all of their insurance money. Instead, they performed elaborate funerals whenever possible because their personal reputations and business viability depended on lavish displays. In the case of R. C. Scott, he used advanced technology as the cornerstone of his funeral practice. Funeral directors felt strongly that clients should allow them always to conduct their duties according to their personal standard of excellence. This feeling caused them to be direct and insistent with clients. Given the weak negotiating position of most families and the importance that the African American community placed on the service, the tremendous amount of influence captured by the funeral director is understandable.

As I pointed out earlier, while price was important to the family's choice of a particular funeral director's set of services, there was not true price competition in the industry between funeral homes. Competition was for the initial possession of bodies and reputation. Thus, there were not any competitive pressures to avoid excess capacity, eliminate inefficiencies, or to produce prices at a competitive level (Federal Trade Commission 1977, 123).

African American funeral directors were successful in this industry because they became experts at using ethnicity to promote their business. Their emphasis on tradition, folklore, and ethnicity created a barrier that African American families were not willing to cross, and a standard of excellence that most outside funeral directors felt unable to offer. The carefully orchestrated perception of vast differences between African American funeral directors and everyone else did not depend on technical expertise, but on a careful understanding of ethnicity, an understanding that guaranteed them large cash payments, prestige, respect, and power.

V
African American Insurance Enterprises

INTRODUCTION

To the Public- Whereas, we believe it to be the duty of
every person to contribute as far as is in their power towards
alleviating the miseries and supplying the wants of those of
our fellow beings who through the many misfortunes and
calamities to which human nature is subject may become fit
subjects for charity. And whereas from the many privations
to which we as people of color are subject and our limited
opportunities for obtaining the necessaries of life, many of us
have been included in the number dependent on the
provisions made by the law, for the maintenance of the poor;
therefore as we constitute a part of the public burden, we
have deemed it our duty to use such means as was in our
reach to lessen its weight, among which we have found the
forming of institutions for mutual relief the most practical
and best calculated to effect our object . . . some have
misunderstood the object and the benefit of these societies,
therefore this report is given. [Notice in the Philadelphia
Ledger, March, 1831] (Trent 1932, 6)

African American citizens in the early twentieth century produced
few manufactured products, but the capital they generated was a significant
portion of the United States' economic base. The insurance industry was
the vehicle for this infusion of African American capital. Most African
American-operated industries were small, personal-service firms, such as
barber, catering, cleaning, hairdressing, or bootblack shops. They
required little capital and served primarily local markets. The African
American insurance industry, in contrast, supported the funeral industry,
and this connection allowed funeral establishments to expand beyond the
typical small, personal-service, African American business. Despite the
diverse forms of African American insurance enterprises, they fulfilled a
common need: insurance guaranteed payment for the funeral director. The
African American funeral industry demanded payment up-front, and the
African American community demanded proper burial services. African

Americans wanted a system that produced payments without regard to individual income, social status, religious belief, or moral conviction. African Americans constantly redefined the insurance system until it met their cultural needs. The economic reward for meeting their cultural goals was substantial. Commercial success meant capital formation on a global scale.

African American people purchased $341,000,000 worth of insurance from African American insurance companies in 1938. This was the face value of the policies they purchased or the amount of 'insurance in force.' African American insurance companies held more insurance in force than the individual countries of Brazil, Poland, Mexico, Rumania, Siam, or Yugoslavia (Stuart 1969, 42). In addition, each of these countries had much higher total populations than the African American population in the United States (Table 15). The total amount of insurance purchased by African Americans was even higher than the $341,000,000 figure quoted above because that figure includes only insurance policies held by African American insurance companies. Records of the total amount of insurance purchased by African Americans are unavailable. However, speculations at the time within African American insurance circles estimated that African-American-owned insurance companies carried only one quarter of the insurance purchased by African Americans (Stuart 1940, 43). Even if this gross approximation is low, a conservative estimate suggests that African Americans held at least one billion dollars worth of insurance: an impressive feat for an ethnic group on the economic fringe of society.

Church relief societies were the earliest organizations to provide insurance for African Americans. These mutual aid societies provided a practical way to pay the funeral director. In their early form, mutual aid societies also served as centers of social activities and religious worship. The community and economic responsibilities of church relief societies increased as their insurance systems became more sophisticated. As insurance organizations evolved, they attracted and employed the African American communities' educated elite; they became advocates for better public health conditions; and, as their facilities grew, their offices became visible emblems of their communities' economic pride. In contrast to the African American funeral industry, which operated without competition from white funeral businesses, African American insurance companies faced direct competition from white firms. Yet, by appealing to racial pride and offering a comparable product, they attracted a large segment of the potential business.

Insurance in Force for Various Countries, 1935-1938 Table 15		
Group	Population	Insurance in Force
France	42,000,000	$2,891,422,000
The Netherlands	8,400,000	2,004,470,000
Italy	42,625,000	1,953,109,000
Argentine Republic	12,000,000	500,000,000
Belgium	8,275,000	341,631,320
Negroes in the U.S.	13,891,143	340,000,000
Brazil	41,500,000	179,186,000
Poland	33,500,000	136,389,000
Mexico	18,000,000	102,966,000
Rumania	19,000,000	76,658,000

Source: M. S. Stuart. *An Economic Detour: A History of Life Insurance in the Lives of American Negroes.* New York: McGrath Publishing Company, 1940; reprint, 1969. 42-43.

The earliest white insurance companies followed the pattern of English companies. They wrote large insurance policies (averaging a thousand dollars) with premiums payable either annually or semiannually (Trent 1932, 28). This approach made commercial insurance unobtainable for lower-income groups. African American commercial insurance companies, targeting lower-income households, recognized that the key to competing against the church relief societies and secret fraternal societies, even with a superior product, was a low, weekly payment plan. These arrangements offered the only viable method for the African American community to purchase insurance. The face value of each policy was small, and frequent layoffs caused a high level of policy lapses, but the industry tailored their product to the needs of the African American market. When the major white insurance companies adopted the products and policies of African American insurance companies, they rapidly added new lower-income business to their books.

African American organizations provided security against the cost of disability or death through three distinct institutions: church relief societies, fraternal benefit societies, and life insurance companies or associations. This study investigates each stage separately.

CHURCH RELIEF SOCIETIES

> These societies were embryonic industrial insurance companies of social tendencies. While they provided social interaction in their weekly or biweekly meetings, they also offered some opportunities for employment and paid sick benefits and death claims. (Trent 1932, 12)

Church relief societies were the primary form of self-help in the African American community from 1787 until the late nineteenth century. They provided the principal mode of protection until the last quarter of the nineteenth century when other insurance options became more appealing. There was little distinction between purely benevolent associations and church-affiliated associations. Since social activities revolved around the church, most associations needed their church connections to recruit new members and strengthen the ties between members. Thus, little distinction existed between secular and sacred associations.

Unfortunately, these early insurance societies did not rely on a scientific assessment schedule. Typically, every member paid the same joining fee and the same dues without regard to age, health or income. Given the small amount of dues, a few closely spaced deaths could easily wipe out a small society's capital reserves. Eventually, potential new members would recognize the advancing age of a society's members and refuse to join. As the flow of new members stopped, societies collapsed. For these and many other reasons including mismanagement, many church relief societies became insolvent. However, the enthusiasm members had for their societies remained strong. Every payment was a down payment on self-respect. Their loyalty signified their devotion to the group and quest for salvation, yet salvation could only arrive with death. This loyalty to a dysfunctional social society was similar to the community unity from death rituals discussed earlier in this book. This is an example of the community bonding together for cultural identify and earning self-respect before death through church relief societies. Because of the high failure rate of societies, most people joined more than one society as insurance for the insurance.

Despite the steady number of individual failures, these societies relieved a tremendous amount of economic and social hardship. In 1884, a gathering of societies outlined their impact on the city of Baltimore in the following statement:

> forty of these societies gave an aggregate membership of over 2100. The number varied from sixteen to one hundred and twenty-one, but as a rule were from thirty to sixty. In the whole course of their work, 1400 members had been buried, $45,000 had been paid for funeral expenses, $125,000 had been given as sick dues, $27,000 had been paid to widows by some thirty of these societies. Over $10,700 had been given toward house rent and over 11,300 had been paid for incidental expenses. There had been paid back to members of many societies from unexpended balances, as dividends, a total of over $40,000. The total amount of money handled by all had been nearly $290,000. (Trent 1932, 12)

The leaders in this movement operated without formal training in business or insurance methods. However, they pioneered the methods needed to collect small economic contributions from the economically disadvantaged and then to redistribute them as buffers against economic disasters. These humanitarians attempted to spread a safety net for members on the lowest rung of the economic ladder. By the turn of the century, their rudimentary efforts established a fertile ground for the development of the African American insurance industry. In addition, they began training the personnel needed to run it.

FRATERNAL BENEFIT SOCIETIES

> The call from many was for a life insurance device which offered substantial amounts of protection at low cost on an intelligible and simple basis. Into such an environment and in response to such a call, fraternal life insurance was born. (Kip 1953, 31)

The fraternal insurance society was a nonprofit organization that provided the same types of insurance as commercial companies, but offered their services to a well defined fraternal or social organization. The terms 'fraternal benefit society,' 'fraternal beneficiary society,' or 'fraternal society,' were interchangeable with 'fraternal insurance society.' Although the insurance products were similar to those offered by commercial insurance companies, the organizational structure of fraternal societies made them more attractive in the late nineteenth century to African Americans. The commercial insurance features implied a higher degree of security, yet the fraternal societies retained the inherent social aspect of church relief societies (Kip 1953, 4).

While fraternal societies have a long history as social orders, the fraternal insurance societies redefined the fraternal basis of charitable relief. The first fraternal order imported into America was the Masonic Order in Pennsylvania during 1730 (Kip 1953, 4). In 1849, the Actors Order of Friendship became the first American fraternal society (Kip 1953, 4). American fraternal insurance societies retained the secret ritualistic and social aspects of the fraternal societies, but changed the basis of the society's charitable relief. Relief changed from being need-based to being a privilege contingent upon maintenance of membership dues (Kip 1953, 4). In contrast to the old world fraternal orders that concentrated their charitable relief on the distressed and indigent populations outside their membership, the American societies funneled funds to the needs of their own members. Members' financial condition had no bearing on their qualification for payments.

African American fraternal orders experienced their most rapid growth, largest volume of business, and highest popularity from 1865-1915. They reached their apex between 1900-1910 (Stuart 1940, 13). However, when R. C. Scott purchased the building for his funeral home in 1920, fraternal orders were still very prevalent. He immediately joined twenty-five or thirty associations to extend his influence. An association had to possess the following characteristics before the law recognized it as a fraternal benefit society:

1)   Mutuality and non-profit aspect of the coverage.

2)   Lodge system with ritualistic form of work.

3)   A representative form of government. (Kip 1953, 5)

The first characteristic relates to the commercial insurance component of fraternal insurance societies. The requirement that fraternal insurance societies have mutuality and a nonprofit status made their insurance operations comparable to any mutual life insurance company, with one exception. Most states required mutual life insurance companies to calculate their surplus profit and distribute this profit to their policyholders or stockholders. However, the legal system never addressed the proper distribution of profits from fraternal insurance societies. This made sense in the early days of fraternal insurance because surplus profits did not exist.

The original method of collecting fees used by the fraternal societies was a level, uniform levy on a postmortem basis. This fee collecting system required every member to pay an equal amount upon the death of any member without regard to age, occupation, or health (Kip 1953, 92). There was major resistance within the African American community to insurance operations producing surplus profits. Surplus money provided the opportunity for fraud. In the eyes of many low-income people, payment at anytime other than death was a loan to the insurance company that they could not afford to make. If the society was large and predominantly young, this simple, postmortem levy plan addressed most of the concerns in the African American community. The society collected money only when necessary. If the society was large, either each individual assessment was small or the death payments were substantial. Most important, the society handled money only during the short period between its collection from members and its delivery to the heirs and funeral directors.

While the insurance features helped fuel the growth of fraternal societies, the social aspects of the fraternal orders nourished their popularity. M.S. Stuart, the vice-president and Director of Governmental Relations for the Universal Life Insurance Company in Memphis, Tennessee, and historian for the National Negro Insurance Association, identified three social features that attracted large crowds to African American fraternal societies in the early years:

1)   The love for the spectacular, the gaudy, flashy colors, the illusions of the tinseled grandeur in the showy and pompous ceremonies.

2)   The natural human craving to take part in affairs governmental and political.

3)   A desire for the advantages of the deep secrets of the

lodges. (Stuart 1940, 11)

The brilliant regalia worn by the African American State Militia during reconstruction became an integral part of African American fraternal societies. The community distinguished most fraternal societies by their flashy uniforms. These uniforms established each organization's identity and were the main attractions in parades and processions connected with holiday celebrations, excursions and funerals. Again the community used a set of rituals and clothing to create solidarity among diverse individuals: a form of solidarity that increased the individual status of group members versus nongroup members. At all public occasions, parades became an integral part of the festival and provided regional networking. Ambitious individuals soon realized that joining fraternal societies were essential for social position and status.

Despite the Southern racial tension at the turn of the century, railroad companies catered to the fraternal societies by giving these groups complete trains. These trains transported whole communities to distant cities on excursions sponsored by different fraternal societies. The railroad companies charged exceedingly low rates and nearly always filled the trains (Trent 1932, 14). A. D. Price sponsored several railroad excursions from Richmond to Seaside Park on Virginia's oceanfront. They might travel from city to city, but usually the trains brought people from the rural sections of the South into the large cities. Enormous parades provided gaiety and fun, and a main feature of every event was the rivalry between fraternal orders. The fraternal societies constantly competed to see which fraternal society had the flashiest uniforms and made the best impression in each parade. Excursions typically began early in the morning; participants enjoyed the festivities all day, and returned late in the night. The two most popular excursion destinations in the South were Atlanta and Richmond (Trent 1932, 14; Waite 1940, 102). In addition, communities judged the status of individuals by the number of fraternal societies represented in their funeral procession, or, in other words, by how many societies they had joined. Therefore, the social functions of fraternal societies contributed to their popularity and their spectacular growth.

White commercial insurance companies emerged during the same period as fraternal insurance companies. In 1875, the larger white commercial insurance companies, led by Prudential Insurance Company of Newark and the Metropolitan of New York, began competing with the fraternal insurance societies for African American business (Trent 1932, 15). After adopting the weekly and monthly payment schedules pioneered by African American insurance organizations, the commercial insurance companies made substantial inroads into the African American and low-income markets. Yet, their penetration into the African American market came to an abrupt stop in 1881. Before 1881, white commercial insurance companies wrote African American insurance polices on the same basis as whites. They had the same benefits and payout. However, in 1881 after a careful investigation, the Prudential Insurance Company sent the following circular to its superintendents and agents about African American risk:

Newark, N. J., Mar. 10, 1881.

To Superintendents and Agents:

The following changes will be made with respect to colored persons (Negroes) applying for insurance in this company under policies issued on and after the week commencing Monday, March 28, 1881. (This applies to all applicants taken during the week commencing Monday, March 21.)

First. Under adult policies the sum assured will be one-third less than now granted for the same weekly premiums.

Second. Under infantile policies, the amount assured will be the same as now but the weekly premiums will be increased to five cents.

These changes are made in consequence of the excessive mortality prevailing in the class above named. They do not apply to other persons. Policies issued prior to March 28 will not be affected by this regulation. Rate tables for use with colored applicants will be duly sent to you. Agents using infantile applications in which the question of race is not asked should write on the lower margin on the back of the application, the word "white" or "colored" as the case may be. Unless this is done, application will be returned for correction.

John F. Dryden, Secretary.

(Trent 1932, 16)

Illustrated in table 16, are the rates tables Dryden sent. Following the change of circumstances at Prudential, many white, commercial insurance companies went further and canceled African American insurance policies outright. These hostile actions toward the African American community served as a catalyst to attract leading African American entrepreneurs into the insurance market. They began attaching insurance components to societies already in existence and eventually began their own African American insurance companies.

Rates of the Prudential Insurance Company of America, 1881 Table 16a				
Age	Weekly Premiums			
	5 Cents		10 Cents	
	White	Colored	White	Colored
13	117.17	78.00		
15	113.00	76.00		
20	103.00	68.00	206.00	
25	90.50	60.00	181.00	
30	79.00	52.00	158.00	
35	67.75	45.00	135.00	
40	56.75	37.00	113.50	
45	45.5	30.00	91.00	
50	37.00	24.00	74.00	
55	29.75	19.00	59.30	
60	23.25		46.50	
65	17.00		34.00	
70	12.5		25.00	
75	9.50		19.00	

Rates of the Prudential Insurance Company of America, 1881 Table 16b				
Age	Weekly Premiums			
	25 Cents		50 Cents	
	White	Colored	White	Colored
13				
15				
20				
25	452.50	300.00		
30	395.00	260.00		
35	338.75	225.00		
40	283.75	185.00		
45	227.50	150.00	455.00	300.00
50	185.00	120.00	370.00	240.00
55	148.75	95.00	297.50	190.00
60	116.25	75.00	232.50	150.00
65	85.00	55.40	170.00	
70	62.50	40.00	125.00	
75	47.50		95.00	

Source: W. J. Trent, Jr. "Development of Negro Life Insurance Enterprises." Master of Business Administration Thesis, University of Pennsylvania, 1932. 16.

Fraternal societies used two race pride issues to recruit members into their insurance organizations. First, they publicized attitudes exhibited by white agents toward their African American policyholders. Besides the large commercial insurance companies that accepted African American clients, there were many small white insurance companies in the South that catered solely to African American and poor white clients. While preying upon the ignorance of their clients by charging exorbitant rates, they had reputations for insulting African American policyholders, especially African American women, during their collection visits (Trent 1932, 29).

> Because of the participation of a white agent in the lynching of a colored man in a southern state, the debit of a struggling Negro company was increased more than 800 per cent within

a month. In another instance, the collection book of a white agent was found "under the lynchtree" in Vicksburg, Mississippi. He lost 60 per cent of his debit and his company a large part of its Negro business in that city. Other instances of the deliberate violation of the privacies of boudoirs and bathrooms over the protests and to the embarrassments of the female inmates have been bitterly and publicly resented by Negro leaders, and effectively used by Negro agents. (Stuart 1940, 36-37)

The second race pride issue focused on respectable jobs. African American insurance organizations created decent jobs for the new stream of African American college graduates. Even in 1928, when the Metropolitan Life Insurance Company had $960,000,000 worth of insurance on more than one million African Americans, they would not employ a single African American to represent the company (Waite 1940, 111).

Despite all the questionable practices that African Americans had to tolerate if they insured with a white insurance company, African American insurance companies presented their own set of problems. M. S. Stuart, historian for the National Negro Insurance Association, gives nine reasons in his book *Economic Detour* why, despite the popularity of fraternal insurance societies, there was almost a general failure of African American fraternal societies:

1)   Inadequate assessments of the insurance departments.

2)   Ignorance of the principles of life insurance.

3)   Mismanagement.

4)   Careless and incompetent selection of the risks.

5)   Political controversy, intrigue, and litigation.

6)   The numerous diversions and detractions of this modern age.

7)   The availability to Negroes of life insurance supplied by pure life insurance companies, without the loss of time and

the trouble of attending lodge meetings.

8)   "Freezing" of the order's funds in big and unnecessary
       building.

9)   Fraud. (Stuart 1940, 15)

Stuart exhibited an elitist and condescending attitude in outlining the
reasons for failure. One suspects that he followed Du Bois' doctrine that
only the talented tenth should be in business. The other 90 percent of the
insurance companies simply tarnished the reputation of the industry.
Nevertheless, I agree with his identification of inadequate assessments,
unnecessary building, and fraud as key reasons for failure.

The flat postmortem assessment initially used by fraternal insurance
societies was uncomplicated because

a society could not owe more than it could pay, for it only
owed and promised to pay what it could collect. (Kip 1953,
93)

Yet, if the society did not experience constant growth while the levies
remained the same, the frequency of those individual levies increased as
the society got older. Faced with many levies in a short period, many
existing members became financially unable to continue their payments.
After learning the society had an aged membership, potential new members
declined to join. Most potential members found the high initial financial
obligations unattractive. This type of plan only worked when other
obligations, beyond the insurance feature, united the members.

Many fraternal societies built large office buildings to symbolize
their strength and prosperity. This was a common goal of many societies.
However, in the late nineteenth century few enterprises needed African
American office space. Most of these buildings never had a chance of
collecting a reasonable amount of rent and assuredly not enough rent to pay
a mortgage. In the end, these assets had few potential buyers. Thus, the
buildings constantly drained the treasuries and had small potential of being
converted back to cash. Richmond's fraternal societies avoided
overbuilding because of the city's large funeral businesses. The funeral
directors stepped in and built multi-story buildings to supply the fraternal
societies' meeting needs and the needs of their funeral businesses. The
funeral business covered the building's expenses. Rental income from the

fraternal societies not only provided supplemental income for the funeral directors, but reduced the cash outlay and debt accumulation of the city's fraternal societies. These actions strengthened the economic foundations of Richmond's societies and of the city. Table 17 lists the fraternal buildings that passed out of African American ownership by 1940 (Stuart 1940, 16-17).

Fraud played a major role in the collapse of fraternal insurance societies. Fraud cost the societies more than the actual dollars misplaced; it also eroded the community's confidence in the ability of African Americans to provide services for themselves. The types of fraud associated with fraternal insurance societies fell into four general categories:

> Misrepresentation of ages; misrepresentation of health conditions; misrepresentation of relationship as to insurable interest; fictitious claims. (Stuart 1940, 18)

In one common fraudulent practice, profit-seekers purchased policies on unrelated older people who were near death. The insured elderly person never knew about the additional policies. The profit-seeker maintained the policy for a short time, and then, upon death, pocketed the insurance payoff. If the policy was current and the person died, it was the duty of the fraternal order to pay up. There were not any age or health restrictions. An elderly person who joined a society paid the same dues as a teenager. If individuals did not care for the social, community, or networking aspects of the fraternal society, the assessment scale encouraged people to apply late in life when their health first began to fade.

Richmond entrepreneurs and religious leaders made substantial contributions to the African American insurance industry. These contributions enabled the companies to accept procedures that introduced scientific methodology into their operations. Several writers, including Dr. Carter G. Woodson, hailed Richmond as the birthplace of African American insurance enterprises (Trent 1932, 21). In 1881, Rev. William W. Browne organized a mixed male and female fraternal beneficiary institution consisting of one hundred people and $150 in cash. The Circuit Court of the City of Richmond granted Rev. Browne a regular charter of incorporation on April 14, 1883. His organization became a joint stock

Repossessed African American Fraternal Buildings, by States, 1940 Table 17		
Building	City	Estimated Cost
Arkansas:		
Mosaic National Temple	Little Rock	$250,000
Mosaic State Annex	"	50,000
Mosaic Hospital	"	100,000
H.L. Bush Bldg & Hotel	"	100,000
Pythian Building	"	100,000
Taborian Building	"	200,000
Sisters of Mysterious Ten and United Brothers of Friendship	"	50,000
Century Life Ins. Co.	"	110,000
Woodmen of Union Bathhouse, Hospital and Office Building	Hot Springs	497,000
Georgia:		
Odd Fellows Building	Atlanta	303,000
Wage-Earners Building	Savannah	100,000
Illinois:		
Pythian Temple Building	Chicago	over 1,000,000
Louisiana:		
Masonic Building	Shreveport	150,000
Court of Calanthe	"	200,000
Mosaic Templar Building	"	50,000
Tennessee:		
Masonic Building	Nashville	150,000
Masonic Building	Memphis	75,000
Taborian Building	"	10,000

Repossessed African American Fraternal Buildings, by States, 1940 Table 17		
Texas: Odd Fellows Building Pilgrims Building	Houston "	387,500 285,000 (Paid Cash 170,000)
True Men and Women of the World	Calvert	85,000
District of Columbia: Masonic Temple	Washington	950,000
Total Loss		5,222,500

Source: M. S. Stuart. *An Economic Detour: A History of Life Insurance in the Lives of American Negroes.* McGrath Publishing Company, 1940; reprint, 1969. 16-17.

company legally known as the "Grand Fountain of the United Order of True Reformers." The True Reformers was the first African American insurance enterprise that constructed an assessment system with age and benefit categorization. Joining fees, policy values, annual dues, and quarterly dues varied according to age and the dollar amount of the policy. The company relied on regular payments and did not require additional levies when members died (Trent 1932, 19-21). Shown in table 18 are assessment tables for three different policy amounts.

The levy system pioneered by the True Reformers set the standard for other insurance enterprises. The True Reformers proved that African Americans would accept regular levies and the possibility of surplus accumulations, if the members felt the levied amounts and payoffs were fair. Although legally defined as a joint stock company, the True Reformers operated as a fraternal order. The three original lodges in 1881 had grown to 2,678 lodges with a membership of more than 100,000 by 1907. This company served as a scientific, intellectual, and cultural bridge to African American commercial insurance companies.

The True Reformers' Class Department Rate Table, 1885 Table 18a					
Class "B" Table					
Ages	Joining Fee	Value of Certificate after 1 yr.	Value of Certificate before 1 yr.	Annual Dues	Quarterly Dues
18-25	$2.50	$200.00	$100.00	$4.75	$1.20
25-30	2.75	200.00	100.00	4.75	1.20
30-35	3.00	200.00	100.00	4.75	1.20
35-40	3.25	200.00	100.00	5.70	1.43
40-45	3.50	140.00	70.00	5.70	1.43
45-50	3.75	115.00	58.00	6.65	1.66
50-55	4.00	90.00	45.00	6.65	1.66
55-60	4.25	65.00	33.00	7.70	1.90

The True Reformers' Class Department Rate Table, 1885 Table 18b					
Class "E" Table					
Ages	Joining Fee	Value of Certificate after 1 yr.	Value of Certificate before 1 yr.	Annual Dues	Quarterly Dues
18-25	$5.00	$500.00	$250.00	$12.60	$3.15
25-30	5.25	500.00	250.00	12.60	3.15
30-35	5.50	500.00	250.00	15.60	3.90
35-40	5.75	500.00	250.00	15.60	3.90
40-45	6.00	500.00	250.00	20.48	5.12
45-50	6.25	500.00	250.00	20.48	5.12
50-55	6.50	500.00	250.00	23.48	5.87

The True Reformers' Class Department Rate Table,1885 Table 18c				
Class "M" Table				
Ages	Joining Fee	Value of Certificate	Annual Dues	Quarterly Dues
18-30	$11.00	$1,000.00	$21.00	$5.25
30-35	12.00	900.00	25.56	6.39
35-40	12.50	900.00	25.56	6.39
40-45	13.00	800.00	26.04	6.51
45-50	13.50	700.00	26.04	6.51

Source: W. J. Trent. "Development of Negro Life Insurance Enterprises." Master of Business Administration Thesis, University of Pennsylvania, 1932. 19-20.

AFRICAN AMERICAN INSURANCE COMPANIES

The younger generation, having the advantage of more extensive educational facilities began to frown upon the management of these fraternal benefit societies and declined to become affiliated. At the same time, these younger men and women recognized the value of insurance coverage and they, together with some of the older persons set about to offer such coverage, deleting the display and secrecy attraction. The appeal to membership was solely on the basis of a soundly run company, regularly chartered that took care in the selection of its risks. These companies appeared just about the time that the fire and zeal for fraternals had been rudely jolted by the failures of numerous among them. The Southern Aid Society and Richmond Beneficial Society of Richmond, Virginia, founded in 1893 and 1894 respectively, are illustrations in point. (Trent 1932, 30)

The turn of the century marked the beginning of the commercial African American insurance companies. A few church relief societies and fraternal societies recognized the demands of the African American community for a more sophisticated and secure mechanism of providing death benefits. These enlightened societies converted into mutual or stock companies, but this conversion saved few from failing, including the True Reformers. The prototype African American insurance companies in this period started as mutual companies owned by the policyholders or stock corporations. They operated unencumbered by social expectations. Many eventually organized as legal reserve companies for added stability. Again, the most successful companies looked to Richmond entrepreneurs and funeral directors for inspiration and guidance.

The oldest and second oldest African American commercial insurance companies in the country were organized in Richmond, Va.: The Southern Aid Society of Virginia, Incorporated and The Richmond Beneficial Life Insurance Company, respectively (Stuart 1940, 230-1). In the midst of fraternal societies' enormous popularity, four Richmond entrepreneurs gambled that as the community became more educated, it would prefer a stand-alone superior insurance product over an inefficient one surrounded by pomp and circumstance. On February 25, 1893 Rev. Z. D. Lewis, Funeral Director A. D. Price, and the Jordan brothers chartered the Southern Aid and Insurance Company. Before founding Southern Aid, the Jordan brothers worked for the True Reformers. The original capital stock was $5,000 and divided into shares of ten dollars (Stuart 1940, 231; Trent 1932, 32).

The business experienced slow growth until the stockholders elected A. D. Price, a founder and board member, as the third president of Southern Aid in January 1905 (*Richmond Planet* 1905, 28 January). In 1906, the company changed its name to the Southern Aid Society of Virginia, Inc. While the company never conducted business as a lodge or fraternal order, the new name resembled names for those types of organizations. Although the Southern Aid Society was not a fraternal order, Price still wanted his insurance company to exploit the popularity of fraternal societies. As a member of 32 fraternal orders at his own death in 1921, funeral director A. D. Price understood fraternal societies and the needs of their members. Southern Aid Society managed its affairs very conservatively and experienced strong growth. The company grew from first year revenues of $7,000 using ten employees to annual collections of more than $500,000 and 300 employees by 1937. Southern Aid paid $7,569,151.76 to its policyholders during this period (Stuart 1940, 232).

The Southern Aid Society served as the model for many new firms in the period, including the North Carolina Mutual and Provident Association of Durham, North Carolina. North Carolina Mutual is still in existence today and was the first African American insurance company to pass the one billion-dollar mark for insurance in force. The company achieved this feat in 1971. The humble beginning of this company occurred in 1898, when seven African American entrepreneurs came together in Durham with the expressed purpose of imitating Richmond's insurance companies:

> Merrick presided over the meeting and declared its purpose was to devise a means "to aid Negro families in distress"; thus "an insurance association similar to the two organized by Negroes in Richmond in 1893 [Southern Aid Society of Virginia] and 1894 [Richmond Beneficial Life Insurance Company] should be organized in Durham." (Weare 1973, 30)

The conservative Southern Aid Society limited its operations to Virginia and the District of Columbia during the first half of the twentieth century.

Richmond's entrepreneurs and funeral directors exhibited their business skill and political power again during the reorganization of the National Benefit Life Insurance Company. In 1898, S. W. Rutherford, a former deputy with the True Reformers, founded a mutual aid fraternal society in Washington, D.C. This company was the United States's largest African American insurance company in 1930 (Trent 1932, 57). Starting as an assessment association with $2,000 in capital, by 1928, the National Benefit had become a legal reserve company with more than forty million dollars of insurance in force. Unfortunately, National Benefit expanded too quickly. It attempted to serve a total of 26 states in 1923 by adding nine new states simultaneously and lavishly equipping the many sub offices. The final misstep was reinsuring the Standard Life Insurance Company in an attempt to save Standard Life from collapsing. Bloated with under-secured loans, overvalued real estate, and employee irregularities, National Benefit collapsed. The courts of the District of Columbia appointed white receivers in March 1932. Out of this carnage emerged the Virginia Mutual Benefit Life Insurance company (Stuart 1940, 315-19; Trent 1932, 46).

> When the National Benefit Life Insurance Company was adjudged insolvent on September 9, 1931, and it became apparent that the general receivers would not take any steps to reorganize the company; when the other twenty-five states in which the National Benefit operated took no action in protest of the unsympathetic attitude of the general receivers; and when even the majority of the policyholders seemed resigned to the ultimate loss of their company--in this vista of gloom--there appeared only one star of hope, and that was in the sky of Old Virginia, when it was announced that the policyholders there had taken independent action to protect their interests by organizing the Virginia Mutual Benefit Life Insurance company to reinsure the business in that state. (Stuart 1940, 238)

Virginia accomplished this feat because Richmond's African American entrepreneurs had the insurance expertise, economic power, and the political connections of funeral director R. C. Scott.

When receivers take over an insurance company, it is uncertain whether policyholders will collect any funds from the previous owners. In addition, the receivers might squander the remaining assets. At the time the receivers took over the National Benefit Life Insurance Company, the company had $3,700,000 worth of assets. The former National Benefit Life president alleged the following in his suit six years later:

> the receivers had collected an additional $1,500,000 and had disposed of all of the company's assets, including the money collected by the receivers, with the exception of $353,000. None of this money, Risher pointed out to the court, had been paid out to policyholders. All of the money sent went to administrative expenses and fees for the receivers and their lawyers. (Stuart 1940, 319)

The Circuit Court of the City of Richmond insisted on an absolute receivership, instead of an ancillary one. The court specifically directed the Virginia receivers to continue the business as an ongoing business. These actions effectively blocked Virginia policyholder funds from leaving the state. This legal protection allowed a group of African American entrepreneurs to organize 95% of the Virginia policyholders into a new and separate insurance company. These policyholders had paid more than

$10,000 in premiums. After reorganization, the Richmond entrepreneurs named the new company the Virginia Mutual Benefit Life Insurance Company, Inc. (Stuart 1940, 238-39; Scott 1957, 26).

The success of the reorganization depended on the attitude and consideration of Judge Julien C. Gunn of the Circuit Court of the City of Richmond, under whose jurisdiction the receivership fell. Judge Gunn, tap dancer Bill "Bojangles" Robinson and funeral director R. C. Scott were close friends. When Booker Talmadge Bradshaw, a top sales agent who managed the state of Virginia for the former National Benefit Life Insurance Company, brought the reorganization plan to Judge Gunn, it appears that R. C. Scott's relationship with Judge Gunn greatly influenced his favorable reaction. Bradshaw had a B. S. degree in Life Insurance from the University of Illinois and eventually became the president of Virginia Mutual. Bradshaw brought in H. A. M. Johns and Clarence Lee Townes as vice presidents. Both had previously worked for the Southern Aid Society and National Benefit Life Insurance companies. Judge Gunn believed in R. C. Scott and the African American insurance industry. Remarkably, he backed up this belief by rejecting the normal practice of only assigning white receivers for African American companies. He appointed R. C. Scott and S. W. Robinson, Jr. as African American receivers. They shared this distinction with the Honorable Leon M. Bazile, Judge of the 15th Judicial District of Virginia, W. H. Cardwell, Attorney and Examiner of Records of the 10th Judicial District of Virginia and John H. Dinneen, Jr., an attorney and insurance expert. Since the receivers eventually became the board of directors, Judge Gunn had the distinction of creating the first integrated insurance company board in the United States according to Scott. Scott later became the chair of the board's finance committee and ultimately chairperson of the Board. Virginia Mutual grew dramatically. At the end of its first five years of existence, the company claimed assets of $58,532. The amount paid out to satisfy sick, accident, and death claims totaled $71,751 (Stuart 1940, 238-43).

SUMMARY

The African American insurance industry provided service to the community through three distinct organizations. Each organization evolved in response to the social, environmental, and economic constraints imposed on the African American community. The church relief societies operated as auxiliary units to the only institution the community controlled. They reinforced the need for mutual assistance as a survival technique and they instilled moral codes. Fraternal societies took over social and economic activities from the church. While insurance features were a small part of what fraternal societies provided their members, the fraternal societies' overwhelming popularity exposed many African Americans to more sophisticated insurance methods. Fraternal societies increased the probability of cash payments to the funeral director. African American commercial insurance companies developed from the unique foundations of the first two insurance organizations. This foundation allowed them to compete successfully against white companies in the first half of the twentieth century. They carved out a niche in the marketplace and delivered a comparable or superior product.

Because African Americans purchased at least one billion dollars worth of insurance by the end of the 1930s and because African American insurance companies carried at least $340,000,000 of this insurance, this industry played a significant role in the capital formation of the United States and provided economic development resources for the African American community. The funeral director was the primary funnel into the community and banking system for this capital. While we cannot figure out exactly what percentage of the more than one billion dollars flowed through the funeral industry, it is undeniable that the funeral directors had first claims on this money and got their share before all others. The court system guaranteed their preferential treatment. The money accumulated in this industry was astounding, especially considering that the source of funds came from a very poor segment of the American population. Yet, given the cultural importance attached to funeral practices, only an industry that supported funeral directors and death rituals could achieve such success during this period in history.

VI
The Funeral of Brother Jesse Harding

This study uses a variety of distinctive sources and techniques to show the power of death rituals in the African American community and their influence on the community's economic development. Yet, this study fails to show how the vast connections between rituals, religion, and business come together to affect the everyday lives of common folks in the community. When community members disagree with the cultural norms of the community and their beliefs are in direct contrast to their minister's expectations, how do they become willing partners in this cultural process?

The following article is an account of the funeral sermon and events surrounding the death of Jesse Harding. His death occurred in the 1920's, in Macon County, Alabama. The church scene illustrates a culturally-dictated dilemma faced by Southern preachers. Southern culture demanded a proper burial for all members of the community no matter what their station in the community. However, the citizens of Macon County were very reluctant to extend to Jesse Harding this cultural right. Also, this account displays the special relationship between the minister and his congregation.

The preacher calls attention to the three major innovations introduced by A. D. Price and R. C. Scott: embalming, advanced technology, and insurance. He illustrates the importance of each innovation in the lives of his congregation and how widespread these innovations were in the African American community. I believe this account exemplifies the interlocking relations surrounding death rituals in the African American community and how they affected the community's everyday members. [The following essay is reproduced from *Shadow of the Plantation*, pages 162-170 by Charles S. Johnson. The University of Chicago Press published this book July 1934.]

Jesse Harding, although a landowner, was not well liked in the community. He belonged to a family of landowners founded by his father many years ago. There are a few others in the community who own land, but Jesse Harding was a fairly successful farmer and above all a good business man. He did not share the spirit of the community in which, even

151

in the aggregate, there was little property. He was honest, straightforward, paying his own debts and exacting payment of debts to him. During the war he had been drafted and carried to France. It gave him a chance to get away from the community. The people came to the funeral, but there was neither praise of his life nor sorrow over his passing. All the devices of the preacher failed to stir them to any of the usual demonstrations of grief which even strangers may command, or to participate in the ceremony with any sort of unction.

At about three o'clock on Sunday the bell began to toll. It was the signal that the procession was moving to the church. The crowd that had been sitting around since the morning service, chatting and eating, jumped up and crowded around the windows and doors to watch the approach of the body and the mourners. Those who had been waiting outside began pushing in for seats, and there was much talking and gossiping, most of which was about the deceased. The preacher came in, showing traces of both excitement and anger. Mounting the rostrum, he raised his hands, but the tumult continued. Then he spoke: "Everybody hush your mouths. You ain't at no frolic; you're at a funeral. Now don't nobody talk. We ain't at no corn-shucking. You all talk like you at a moving picture show." His remarks had been ill chosen, for there was tittering over his reference to frolics and picture shows. He tried another appeal. "Be quiet, please. Don't talk. Sh....Who's that talking over there, and I told them to stop talking? If white folks had a been in here you could a heard a pin drop." This was not only a warning by suggestion; it was a confession. The shadow of the plantation extended even into their most intimate institutions.

Quiet followed, but whether from fear or shame or satiety was not clear. The preacher continued: "Now you know we will have to have two or three seats here for the family. You all (pointing to a group before him) just move out, please, and let the family have these front seats." Having settled his audience, he picked up his Bible swiftly and stumbled down the aisle to meet the family and the corpse, now waiting at the door. He found them and started back with hardly a pause, leading them to the front, chanting solemnly:

> Man that is born of a woman is few days and full of trouble. He cometh forth like a flower....[everybody stand up]....and is cut down. He fleeth also as a shadow and continueth not, etc....

The choir sang:

> There is rest for the weary
> On the other side of Jordan,
> There is rest for me.

The preacher spoke again. "I'm going to ask you all once more to please give the family all the front seats...."

> When I come to die....

He carried these last words smoothly into a spiritual:

> I want to be ready, I want to be ready,
> To walk in Jerusalem just like John.

A deacon offered up a perfunctory and almost completely stereotyped prayer, during which the pastor shouted several times, "You better pray," and the audience responded with low and doleful moans, more like a learned song than the spontaneous expression of feeling. Another song, "Beautiful land of God," and the preacher announced: "We are going to spend about ten minutes to have Brother Wiley and Brother Saunders to say a few words. The family has asked that they say a few words, and I will give them just about three minutes each." Brother Saunders arose briskly. He was one of the few persons of the community who had known the deceased well and could appreciate his curious objectives in life.

> Pastor, Members, and Friends of Damascus Baptist
> Church: I have known this young man practically all his life.
> He stayed right here and was with us all the time. I can say
> this young man was a real man; you know you can't say this
> about all men and women, but he was a real man; a man that
> was worth while. He served his country and that was the
> cause of his death. Mr. Harding was a real business man; he
> didn't play' he didn't believe in no foolishness. If you want
> to do business with him it was all right, but if you went for
> foolishness he didn't have no time for you, and everything he
> said was just about true. You could believe him if you
> wanted to, but what he said was so. I come to see him last
> Wednesday a week ago, and we set down on the porch and

talked; I with him and him with me. He started to talk about death, and I told him that death would take care of itself, and I started talking about something else. He said "Let's talk about death, because you know I got to go 'cording to the Scripture. I got to go to another building, and you know I got to go." I want to say to you all, be you a man or a woman, if you live for something you will die for something.

The audience had listened only half heartedly, restlessly, and with none of the emotions which a funeral is expected to evoke. Brother Wiley sensed this, and, after a brief allusion to the coldness, made a very perfunctory remark and sat down without further endangering his standing with the audience. He said: "This seems to be a mighty quiet funeral. You don't find many of our funerals so quiet. We are here on a very sad occasion. I been knowing Brother Jesse for a long time, and we thought a lot of him in this community." The preacher felt a challenge to his greatest skill in arousing this audience to the appropriate feeling for such an occasion. But he had great difficulty in finding words. His sermon offers a remarkable example of forced movement, from the platitudes of the beginning to the artificial "rousements." "Friends, this is a very sad occasion," he reminded them again. "Brother Jesse was converted under Rev. Dr. Banks, who has gone on to heaven." Still getting his bearings: "Brother Wiley and Brother Saunders had given you some very good talks." The chill of the audience bore down upon him, and he admitted, almost bargainwise: "Brother Jesse had his faults, like you and me. I talked with him at home and at the hospital." He excused himself for not visiting him at the hospital oftener: "They had to ask me to not come to the hospital so much, 'cause there was so many sick folks just like Brother Jesse." Everybody knew the deceased's forthrightness and it could be mentioned again.

> Brother Jesse was the business man of the Harding family. The old man was lucky before them; all of that family has been lucky. He was a keen business man. If you went to ask him about a certain thing, and he tell you ain't nothing to it, it wasn't nothing to it, and that's all there is to it.

Then, reading the faces of his audience, he faced the issue squarely:

I know you all waiting to see what I'm going to say. Brother Jesse told me, and not only me but others, that he didn't go to church as often as he ought to have. But God has forgive him for that. I'm saying this for the other young men here that ain't been to church before this year. God ain't gonna love you. Jesse didn't go to church as he ought to have, but I tell you one thing he did do. He would pay what he owed and he would give a receipt for everything, and he would give a receipt when you did business with him. He was a business man, somehow or other.

There are other virtues implied in his life which came closer to the general community notions of respectability. "He died and left his wife in good shape. Left her his home; left her not begging; left her with something around her. She's crying now but she ain't crying 'cause she ain't got nothing to eat." It was this thrust by the preacher which brought the first response. The audience quieted for a while as if stunned, and the preacher indulged in a few easy personal reminiscences.

He always made me welcome in his home. He not only invited me there to breakfast or dinner one time, but all the time whenever he would see me he would ask me if I wouldn't have something to eat with them. He didn't talk no foolishness, but he was a business colored man; he had sho-enough visible long eyes.

Then, addressing the corpse, he said: "Jesse, we are going to talk from the text we used to talk about. For we know this is a building of God not made with hands eternal in the heavens.'" At this point the sermon was interrupted by the singing of an old hymn. The widow arose and walked around the casket, waving her hand in farewell at the remains and crying, "Goodbye, goodbye, I am all by myself now; ain't got nobody, Lord, nobody but me and myself." A friend came up and began fanning her. By the end of the song the preacher had better command of himself, and launched into his sermon, deliberately and with determination.

When we are about to build a house the architect makes out all the plans and states the number of things it takes to go into the making of the building. We go according to the directions that he gives us. Bad disaster of a serious kind, rainstorms, and what not comes along and destroys it, and it goes back to the dust from whence it came. The upkeep is always more expensive than the building. To build a building and not have the upkeep is a waste of time, material, and money. Time after time somebody had to go around to look after the building to keep it up. Brother Harding had to go make preparations for another building. When God created heaven and earth he had nothing to start with; he had no material. He planted the world while the world was dark. He didn't have nobody to pull up by, nobody but himself. That is the kind of protection Jesse had. When you got your hands in God's hand you don't need to worry. In Indiana once I went down to visit a building that took ninety-nine years to finish-just lack one year of taking a hundred years to build. But that building is going to rot down; time is going to wear it out. Storms and rains is going to tear it down after a while. Jesse's government sent him over in France. He got gassed and gas got all through his body, but he done it for me and you. He is saying, "All you can do for me, Mr. Hoover, now is give me a home over yonder. Got to go back and have a home when the government done signed up. Gonna need one after a while."

The creation of the world by God out of nothing is one of the most powerfully dramatic incidents in time and space. It provides an opportunity for imagery of the most effective sort, and is colored with a deep and eternal mystery. It was this picturization that the preacher resorted to by way of awakening his audience.

God talked, and one thousand birds came from nowhere. He talked and the waters of the deep come gushing up. [I got to hurry on now.] Jesse begin to breathe the breath of life. When God breathe the breath of life in you, you are going to know it. Noah built the ark, but I'm talking about this house not made with hands. Old house built upon the sand give away some time. You can't live in a house when it gets too shaky. Old disease got in Jesse's house and he couldn't live. Brother Jesse's heart can't move no longer 'cause disease got in it. Mrs. Jesse heard Jesse talking to someone but she couldn't see who it was. God was telling him to come on in. Jesse said, "Take me and keep me out of my misery." He was talking to someone but none could see who it was but Jesse could see. When T. B. get into your body you can't stand it. All right, Jesse, all right, all right, boy, do the best you can; I ain't gonna cry no more. Don't cry everybody has done all they could. Jesse gone and left us all. He said, "I am fixing for another world; the things of this world won't do me no good. I will meet you over yonder after a while." They tell me that if you believe in the word of God, he will save you in the dying hour. When he was converted he asked what they meant when they said, "Believe on God and keep his commandments." Brother Tate told him to just believe in the word of God, and trust him and turn loose and a power from on high would do the rest. O man, O man, after a while the old Kaiser said, "I believe I will go down here in France and play the old devil with the young boys." Jesse went over there with a bunch of boys from here; some was with the mechanics and some was on the firing line. The old Kaiser played the devil with our boys. I can imagine I can hear Jesse praying to come back home. He didn't have no wife then. O Lord, O Lord, O, it got so dark then in France, they say one time they was digging graves 138 hours, burying men who had fallen in France. Brother Jesse didn't happen to fall in that crowd, but he had to stand in water up to his knees. He told me once he didn't see how he got that disease, and I told him that he brought it back from France; that he caught it over there. I told him not only him but there was thousands of other boys in the same condition. He went in there one evening and got on the scales and he had lost seven or eight pounds, and the next week they put him on the scales again and he had lost about eight and a half pounds, and he said, "I can't stay here long going away like this." After a while he got to meet that monster Death. At the hospital they weigh you to see how you are getting along. All that is over with you now, boy. You ain't gonna stand in line no more. We won't see him no more going to see after the stock in the barn. O man, I will meet you after a while. I fancy Jesse talking to his father, and him asking about all of the children down here. O wife, you won't have to walk around the bed giving him medicine no more. O Lord, O Lord! O Jesus, take care of us! I imagine I can see Jesse walking in Jerusalem just like John. Ain't got on no soldier's clothing, ain't got on no gas mask; but he's got on the helmet of salvation, sitting around God's throne.

The congregation was now partially aroused. They began humming and moaning loud enough at time to cross the words of the minister, but without force or spontaneity. "You all sing mighty sorry," the preacher chided. "You act like you can't sing." Then noticing some of the members stealing out, he shouted: "Don't nobody go out. Don't nobody go out over the corpse." Another song was started and four women accommodatingly shouted "Lordy, Lordy" and ceased promptly with the music. Once more the preacher attempted a figure: "Jesse, you are not over the council of Daniel, of John, of Amos. We will meet again. We will meet over yonder. Jesse's wife comes first." At mention of her name, the wife began crying aloud again, "O Lord, I ain't got nobody; Lord, nobody but me now, Lord."

The preacher observed, sadly:

Jesse can't say nothing, Lord.
I imagine I can hear Amos and John say, "I wonder where my mother is." Jesse will see them soon, and say, "I'm troubled, Lord; I'm troubled." Jesse ain't going to cry no more; he ain't going to tell me about being motherless and fatherless. Don't give up sisters, brothers, and wife. Love each other and live at peace with one another. Amen.
Don't nobody go out. The undertaker will tell you which way to come up and see the body. This body has been embalmed so there ain't nothing to be afraid of. We got a little debt on the pump, so you all put a nickel on the table as you pass to look at the body. Don't talk. Pass quietly, please. Don't talk. Don't go outdoors. Go out behind the body.

O Lordy, let your will be done.
O Lordy, let your will be done.
Says, O Lordy, let your will be done.

If it takes my mother,
Let your will be done.

If it takes my mother,
Let your will be done.

O Lordy, let your will be done.
O Lordy, let your will be done.
O Lordy, let your will be done.

You all ain't dropping no nickels on the table.
On the third Sunday our anniversary will be completed.
Every member of this church ought to be registered. Seems
like you all forgetting to honor the older members of this
church. Now listen here: Sister Harding has lost her
husband, and we realize that, and I want every brother and
sister to console her. Go and throw your arms about her and
help that wife and comfort her. Go over there tomorrow
morning and help her clean up everything....The family will
go down the same aisle they come up.

At the graveyard the Negro undertaker who had come up from
Montgomery was introducing a new device, an automatic lowering
apparatus. The pallbearers were temporarily nonplused, and were lost for
something to do until they were permitted to fill in the grave. The
preacher sang, "I want to walk in Jerusalem just like John," and at the end
of the song announced that he wanted to take the occasion to speak of the
fact that the funeral had been conducted from the house to the grave by a
"member of our race." He called the undertaker, who promptly stepped
forward to acknowledge this recognition. Said the minister:

You can see for yourself he's a shore-enough member
of the race; he's like Brother Thomas over there and we all
agree that he is real dark.
I want to remind you also how necessary it is to keep
up insurances do that you won't be a burden on other people
when you come down to die.

VII
Conclusion

OVERVIEW

This study uses the autobiography of R. C. Scott to begin an exploration into the socioeconomic issues of ethnicity and entrepreneurship in the early twentieth century. My focus on the African American funeral business highlights an industry that successfully operated under the separate but equal doctrine and illustrates the influence of culture on a specific range of entrepreneurial activities. Sheltered from discrimination and racism, African American funeral directors not only survived and surpassed their white counterparts in Richmond, but also created a national fraternity of economic and political elite who wielded significant power in the United States.

The leading African American funeral directors of Richmond, Va., including A. D. Price and R. C. Scott, had a hunger for power and prestige. Despite their gracious manner and devoted service toward their clients, they were shrewd, hustling, and innovative entrepreneurs. They followed the theme of "charity yes, but charity tempered with prudence" (Scott 1957, 18). The community supported this value system by consistently funneling cash into the funeral industry via transportation fees, meeting rentals, insurance organizations, etc.

THE AFRICAN AMERICAN FUNERAL INDUSTRY RECONSIDERED

Funerals, funeral processions, and public ceremonies are political acts and economic events that channel power into African American community. The African American funeral industry capitalized on culture to create community solidarity and provide a monetary foundation for economic development. African American funeral directors cultivated social roles within the community beyond simply providing funeral services. They were business and social leaders. Despite the solicitous professional demeanor of Richmond's major African American funeral directors, A. D. Price and R. C. Scott, they were both contentious and assertive businesspeople.

R. C. Scott built his business on providing the latest technological innovations. His eagerness to incorporate innovations establishes Scott as a contemporary of innovating entrepreneurs such as James Buchanan Duke of American Tobacco Company and Gustavus Swift of Swift & Company, rather than the traditionalist shopkeeper in the African American community. Scott and Price far surpassed both their white and African American local competitors. They measured success against a select group of funeral directors on a national level.

The African American community holds death rituals in high esteem because of their universal acceptance in society, their ability to transform and enhance the status of individuals, and society's acceptance that elaborate funerals are necessary as symbolic statements. These death rituals and the symbolism attached to them are transplants of African death rituals. They are extensions of the elaborate funeral rites used by the Bakongo to secure a pledge of ancestral goodwill. The Bakongo honored the dead and practiced ostentatious funeral rituals as important survival techniques for the living. The African American community held ostentatious funeral rituals to establish the status of the living. In the early twentieth century, goodwill and survival depended on status.

Funeral directors captured a tremendous amount of influence because of the weak negotiating position of most families needing their services and the importance that the African American community placed on the service. They became experts at using ethnicity to promote their business. Their emphasis on tradition, folklore, and ethnicity created a barrier that African American families were not willing to cross, and a standard of excellence that most outside funeral directors felt unable to offer.

The African American insurance industry provided the financial support for the funeral directors' activities. African Americans purchased at least one billion dollars worth of insurance by the end of the 1930's. Most of the insurance money entered the community through direct payments to the funeral director. By channeling large payments to the community, the funeral industry indirectly supported many auxiliary businesses. In the community, death rituals both created a sense of community and provided the economic basis to support that community.

FINAL THOUGHTS

One potential criticism of this analysis is its reliance on surveys, material culture or anecdotal material to support the argument of distinctive cultural-based funeral rituals. A literature search failed to find any studies that could statistically prove the existence of distinctive funeral rituals based on ethnicity. There are studies that quantify funeral customs based on funeral cost (Gebhart 1928; Hoffman 1919; Mitford 1963), but none that statistically validate distinctive cultural-based funeral customs during the early twentieth century. I address this concern in Appendix A by analyzing insurance death payments among whites, blacks and mulattoes (census definitions) in Richmond. In this Richmond study, I statistically validate that funeral preparation is distinctive among various ethnic groups. The amount of insurance held by the white, black, and mulatto subjects in my analysis varied according to ethnicity.

The Richmond analytical study also reveals financial information that can be used to figure out R. C. Scott's financial structure. By using the average African American death payment of $1,779.45 from appendix A, one can estimate that, in 1926 when R. C. Scott averaged more than one funeral a day for the year (*Richmond Planet* 1927, 8 January), the R. C. Scott funeral home grossed approximately $649,335. Based on this type of economic strength in 1926, it is not surprising that Judge Gunn and Scott were friends and Judge Gunn turned to R. C. Scott to integrate the Virginia Mutual Benefit Life Insurance company's board of directors.

R. C. Scott's life is a validation of Booker T. Washington's model for economic nationalism. In business affairs R. C. Scott was a segregationist. He obtained his revenue and clients predominantly from the African American community. However, although he created his wealth within the African American community, this did not preclude him from trading with white funeral directors in private or becoming a close confidant to the white political establishment. R. C. Scott was a segregationist in business dealings but an integrationist in politics.

Du Bois' plan to achieve economic opportunities through political equality failed. Despite the unparalleled political avenues open to ethnic groups today, many ethnic groups are still struggling to bring substantial numbers of their membership to an acceptable economic level. However, in this one rare example of an African American industry that faithfully followed Washington's message, these entrepreneurs achieved the economic and political results Washington prophesied.

This study's reliance on newspaper accounts, an autobiography, and oral interviews will create additional concerns for some researchers reviewing this work. Each of these sources can give a bias or subjective account of events. The newspaper reflects the personal philosophies of the editor, John Mitchell, and selective recall is frequently evident in personal accounts. However, due to the lack of primary source material specifically about African American funeral directors, Scott's previously unpublished autobiography is the most insightful account of an African American funeral director in existence. It exposes an interpretation of the funeral director's role in the African American community that only an autobiography could reveal. Despite the large amount of material gathered from the oral interviews with Richmond funeral directors, I included in this book only those events independently verified in the *Richmond Planet*. If the accounts are subjective, then they are a community perception that has been consistent over time and are the perceptions this document seeks to measure.

FUTURE RESEARCH

The ethnic enclave theory explains why funeral homes could achieve economic and political power on such a ratified level. African American funeral homes guaranteed that nearly all of the African American insurance companies' assets and the policy amounts held by white insurance companies reentered the African American community. Any industry that controlled the placement of approximately one billion dollars in the minority sub-economy commanded social status and political clout. The money circulating through the enclave supported many community businesses. The entire community became financially stronger from the economic stimulus provided by the funeral director as increasing numbers of enclave businesses recycled money within the community and became interdependent. The meeting space provided by Richmond funeral directors for the fraternal organizations, offer a prime example: The funeral home meeting space meant that the fraternal orders did not have to use their capital for building construction costs or lose capital outside the community by renting from white landlords. Therefore, the funeral businesses strengthened the entire Richmond African American community.

I suggest that developing a quantitative ethnic enclave model to compare the interdependency of different African American communities is a promising area for future research. Armed with the interdependencies from various ethnic communities across the country, the researcher could test the correlation of a strong local funeral industry with a high level of interdependency. Potentially, this type of analysis could directly link this Richmond analysis with similar environments throughout the United States.

This study also raises the question of whether circumstances surrounding today's African American death rituals are significantly different from the early twentieth century. By using current insurance industry databases, an investigator can figure out funeral cost by geographic, ethnic, and income dimensions. An industry study will reveal this information without the problems of unrecorded multiple death payments from different insurance companies.

Are funeral directors still major power brokers in the African American community? If they are not, has the lost of power resulted from different economic or cultural circumstances? If they still wield considerable power, how do they administer their power?

This study establishes the economic and social power of funeral directors in Richmond, Virginia. Yet, how did A. D. Price and R. C. Scott use their power in politics and race relations. The Virginia Mutual Life Insurance case illustrates a behind-the-scene political maneuver by Scott, but how frequently did he engage in these activities and what were his strategies? What was the range of exchanges between Price, Scott, and the white political establishment? Did R. C. Scott support the NAACP's legal challenges to segregation or did he support segregation because of its economic potential for African American businesses? Given the breath of R. C. Scott's autobiography, his political views are conspicuously absent, why?

The funeral directors achieved elite status in the African American and white communities by using economic segregation to achieve political integration. The elite status of funeral directors such as R. C. Scott and their willingness to be on the forefront of innovative techniques provides a consistent story about a primary segment of the African American power structure. Regrettably, this segment has not received attention from previous researchers. While one can question whether scholars overlooked these entrepreneurs due to a lack of knowledge, their discovery will force business historians and sociologists to revise their concept of African American entrepreneurship in the early twentieth century.

Appendix A
Richmond Data Analysis

African Americans and whites observe different ethnic-based death customs. In the past, researchers from many disciplines relied on surveys (Crocker 1971; Gebhart 1928; McGee 1981), material culture (Herskovits 1941; Thompson 1983), or anecdotal material (Carawan 1989; Genovese 1976; Puckett 1969) to support their arguments of distinctive cultural-based funeral rituals. While successfully identifying this cultural phenomenon, these studies lack the theoretical framework necessary to validate the distinction statistically. The current study uses a different methodological approach to explore these cultural phenomena. Using insurance as the independent variable, the study provides a statistically valid test of whether different death customs exist between African American and white populations.

In the past, scholars that quantified funeral customs concentrated on funeral cost (Gebhart 1928; Hoffman 1919; Mitford 1963). These funeral cost studies provided background for the authors' comments on the social or economic character of the funeral industry. The studies centered either on the funeral industry's unfair pricing policies (Bowman 1959; Gebhart 1928; Mitford 1963) or on the funeral directors as innocent providers of social services (Habenstein and Lamers 1956; Pine and Phillips 1970; Hohenschuh 1900). These scholars used funeral cost analysis primarily to figure out whether different economic levels or ethnic groups paid disproportionately high funeral amounts to satisfy cultural status needs.

There are three primary factors used to decide funeral expenses: 1) survivors' guilt, 2) family status, and 3) funeral director manipulation. However, each of these primary elements takes place after the death. The deceased rarely had any role in these areas. Culture, ethnicity, and community pressures influence survivors. Therefore, the survivors based the level of funeral expenditures on the family's speculation of what the deceased wanted (Vernon 1970, 10). This appendix analysis filters out these externalities and concentrates on the deceased's value system. I accomplished this by using insurance death payments as the basis for this study. The individual expresses their value system by deciding whether to purchase a life insurance policy for death benefits. The individual also reaffirmed their decision to purchase life insurance over an extended period through annual, monthly, or sometime weekly premium payments. Insurance death policies maintained by the deceased are their statements about the proper level of funeral expenditures and are not subject to speculation or manipulation.

THEORETICAL FRAMEWORK AND HYPOTHESES

By the early twentieth century, the insurance industry developed into a major industry in America (Gebhart 1928, 96). Insurance policies provided most of the death benefits previously dispensed by social and beneficial societies. These policies were also readily available and aggressively marketed in both African American and white communities. In the late nineteenth and early twentieth century, low and middle income citizens, especially African Americans, obtained insurance policies primarily to cover the policyholder's burial expenses. The desire for a proper burial motivated this purchase instead of a concern to provide resources for survivors.

> Lower-class black policyholders seldom conceived of insurance as the middle-class convention of investment and estate-building. Instead, life insurance in the minds of the masses meant burial insurance. Well into the twentieth century the business of black insurance had not divorced itself from the traditions and practices of the early mutual benefit and burial associations, most of which were linked directly to the church. Insurance was more than a profane financial arrangement; it was a folkway. (Weare 1973, 183)

Widely available to African Americans and whites, insurance is a product with few socioeconomic barriers and serves as an acceptable independent variable for this study.

If various American cultures treat death differently, the proportion of individuals holding insurance among diverse ethnic groups in similar economic circumstances should also differ.

Hypothesis 1: The proportion of insurance holders within economically comparable ethnic groups will be different.

By finding the proportion of insurance holders, researchers learn how pervasive insurance is among various ethnic groups; however, this level of analysis is unable to quantify how valuable those policies were to their owners. If individuals purchased insurance to augment the anticipated estate of the policyholder, and the estate represented the material values of the deceased, then the value or importance of the insurance policies can be estimated by the percentage of the total estate made up of death benefits. The larger the ratio of insurance payments to total estate value, the greater the role of insurance in the culture of that ethnic group, assuming similar economic status. The ratio of insurance payments to total estate value reflects the extent of death preparation and the value of that preparation compared with the deceased's lifetime material wealth. This assumption recognizes that lower economic subjects could have a high ratio of insurance payments to total estate value due to their income status. This should not affect the analysis however, since the study compared ethnic group members of similar economic backgrounds.

> Hypothesis 2: The mean ratio of insurance payments to total estate value differs among ethnic groups.

RESEARCH METHODS

The 1910 and 1920 Richmond censuses and estate records from the Chancery Court of Virginia provided the data for this study. I collected the data using the following systematic procedure: 1) a comparable subset of Richmond's black, white, and mulatto population (census classifications) from census enumeration district reports was identified; 2) I found out which members of those populations died before 1927; and 3) upon finding an estate for any individual, I linked the estate information with the census demographic data for statistical analysis.

I sought specific enumeration districts that would produce representative numbers of African-American and white populations from similar economic and social backgrounds. I defined comparable economic and social enumeration districts as neighborhoods that housed blacks/mulattoes and whites with similar occupations such as tobacco factory workers and/or similar housing stock. Initially, I identified 1741 subjects from the 1910 census (497 blacks, 393 mulattoes, and 851 whites) and 1160 subjects from the 1920 census (491 blacks, 409 mulattoes, and 260 whites) for a total of 2901 subjects (988 blacks, 802 mulattoes, and 1111 whites). The initial sampling procedure used only the 1920 census. I modified this procedure to include names from the 1910 census, when the probate court records became unusable after the year 1926 due to an agency indexing problem. The selected subjects were 45 years of age or older. The selection of at least 45 year-old individuals conformed to the life expectancy of African Americans (44.6 years) and whites (58.2 years) in that period (Census of Population, 1910, 1920; Bureau of the Census, 1975), and increased the probability that the subject would have an estate. Those 45-year-old individuals in 1910 were 55 years old by 1920 and had to reach the age of 61 to avoid being eligible for this study, unless they moved out of Richmond. Subjects who were 45 years of age or older from the 1920 census had a smaller probability of being captured in the study than the subjects who were 45 years old in 1910, unless they were 55 years of age or older by 1920.

If we concentrate on the 1910 segment of Richmond's total African American population to avoid capturing individuals in both the 1910 and the 1920 censuses, approximately 15.39 percent of Richmond's total African American population was 45 years of age or older in 1910. Assuming the percentage of African Americans over 45 years of age in the Clay and Henry wards--all of the 1910 enumeration districts chosen were within Richmond's Clay and Henry wards--was the same as Richmond's total African American population (.15387 * 12700 (the total Clay & Henry African American population) = 1954), then the study sampled 45.85 percent of the 1910 African American population over 45 years of age in these wards (497 black & 393 mulatto subjects in the 1910 sample \ 1954 = .458). Using the same methodology, the study sampled 5.43 percent of the white population over the age of 45 in these two wards.

The study matched names of the subjects from the census against names of individuals who died between 1910 and 1926 and filed an estate with the probate court. I identified 171 subjects with estate records from the initial sampling (black 44, mulatto 35, and white 86 cases). The low economic status of the neighborhoods and people (factory workers, drivers, clerks, teachers, and seamstresses, for example) and their probable aversion to the court system, anticipates the low number of subjects found with estates. In addition, the 171 cases originated in a much smaller population than the initial 2901 subjects. While the sampling technique could not identify how many of the 2901 subjects died before 1926, it is logical that the number of people who died and were eligible to have an estate was a small subset of the 2901 people initially identified. The study recorded the value of each estate, the values of all insurance death benefits that were part of the estate, and the number of insurance companies owing money to the estate for each subject with an estate. Out of the 171 estates, 165 had all of the data elements and 35 had some amount of insurance as parts of their estate (black 13, mulatto 14, and white 8 cases).

STATISTICAL ANALYSIS

As shown in the table below, the initial analysis screened the 171 cases for those estates that had insurance payments as part of the estate. Out of the 47 black estates, 27.7 percent contained insurance benefits, 9.1 percent of the 88 white estates contained insurance, and 38.9 percent of the 36 mulatto cases had insurance components. According to hypothesis 1, if culture influences the decision to hold insurance, then each population segment should hold insurance at a different rate. The Chi-square test provides a good base for judging whether the proportions of more than two populations are different. A statistical analysis of this contingency table using a chi-square distribution reveals significant differences in the ownership of insurance among different American ethnic groups (chi sq. = 15.99, df=2, p<.00034). Based on this analysis, we accept hypothesis 1. Culture has a statistically significant impact on decisions about insurance needs. It also influences the way ethnic groups observe death customs.

Survey of 171 Richmond Estates			
RACE	NOT INSURED	INSURED	TOTALS
BLACK #	34	13	47
PERCENT	72.3	27.7	27.5
WHITE #	80	8	88
PERCENT	90.9	9.1	51.5
MULATTO #	22	14	36
PERCENT	61.1	38.9	21.1
COLUMN #	136	35	171
TOTAL %	79.5	20.5	100

CHI-SQUARE	VALUE	DF	SIGNIFICANCE
PEARSON	15.99482	2	0.00034

When comparing the means of more than two populations of ratios, the one-way analysis of variance (ANOVA) is the appropriate statistical tool. This study will accept or reject hypothesis 2 by calculating the ratio of insurance payments to total estates for each population segment. If hypothesis 2 is true, the mean for each population should differ significantly.

The mean ratios of insurance payments to total estate values (165 cases) were .1884 for blacks, .0294 for whites, and .2634 for mulattoes, respectively. The analysis of variance revealed the means were significantly different (F[2,1] = 10.66, p < .0001).

Insurance as a Percentage of Total Estate					
	SUM	MEAN	STD DEV	SUM OF SQ	CASES
BLACK	8.2892	.1884	.3574	5.4914	44
WHITE	2.5265	.0294	.1296	1.4282	86
MIX	9.2183	.2634	.4010	5.4681	35
TOTALS	20.0340	.1214	.2765	12.3876	165

Analysis of Variance					
	SUM OF SQ.	D.F.	MEAN	F	SIG.
BETWEEN GROUPS	1.6313	2	.8156	10.6664	.0001

Based on this analysis, it appears that blacks and mulattoes had a higher rate of insurance possession than whites. If I combined and compared the figures for blacks and mulattoes to those for whites, this still suggests a significant difference between the mean ratio of insurance payments to total estates (F[1,1] = 19.85, p < .0001).

Insurance as a Percentage of Total Estate					
	SUM	MEAN	STD DEV	SUM OF SQ	CASES
BLACK/ MIXED	17.5075	.2216	.3767	11.0691	79
WHITE	2.5265	.0294	.1296	1.4282	86
TOTALS	20.0340	.1214	.2769	12.4972	165

Analysis of Variance					
	SUM OF SQ.	D.F.	MEAN	F	SIG.
BETWEEN GROUPS	1.5216	1	1.5216	19.8466	.0000

Comparing whites to African Americans (blacks/mulattos) is a better comparison because the mulatto designation by the census taker was very subjective. A comparison of African Americans versus whites also provides a comparable number of cases in each population (African American 79, white 86).

A test on the mean ratios of just the 35 cases with insurance payments still show a significant difference between the ratio of insurance payments to total estates when comparing African Americans and whites ($F[1,1]=5.23$, $p<.03$). This difference existed despite African Americans having larger total estates on average ($12,940 for African American estates and $2,653 for white estates).

Insurance as a Percentage of Total Estate				
	SUM	MEAN	STD DEV	SUM OF SQ	CASES
BLACK/ MIXED	17.5075	.6484	.3719	3.5966	27
WHITE	2.5265	.3158	.3172	.7045	8
TOTALS	20.0340	.5724	.3610	4.3011	35

Analysis of Variance					
	SUM OF SQ.	D.F.	MEAN	F	SIG.
BETWEEN GROUPS	.6828	1	.6828	5.2384	.0286

In this analysis of 35 estates with insurance payments, on average 65 percent of the African American estates consisted of insurance payments, compared to a 32 percent insurance component among the white estate cases. Although the significance is not as great as the previous test, due to the small sample size, in each case Hypothesis 2 is accepted.

This analysis could have wider implications and greater statistical impact if the sample population of 171 is a statistically representative sample of the total population (2601). A Chi-square test comparing the sample population (171) and the total population (2601) by sex, marital status, and race produced unacceptably high Chi-squared numbers. Thus, I am unable to claim that the sample population of 171 is a representative sample of the total population.

Yet, the reason the sample is not representative is a structural one and strengthens the analysis. The two areas with high Chi-square numbers are sex and race. The sex category of the sample is overpopulated with males compared with the total population. Since the court listed estates from a husband or wife under the husband's name, estate records were a male dominated information source. Virtually any analysis of estate records will be biased in favor of males. I rejected overpopulating the sample with women because this distorts the reality of cases heard in estate courts. Upon investigating the race component of the sample, the sample is overpopulated with whites. Given that black and mulatto populations had a greater incidence of insurance on a relative and absolute basis, the over sampling of whites strengthens the findings that African Americans placed a greater emphasis on insurance and the need for proper burials.

The analysis of these 171 cases and their results can be specifically applied to Richmond's Henry and Clay wards in 1910 and has implications for the entire city of Richmond. If 34.2 percent (27 African American estates with insurance / 79 total African American estates) of Richmond's 7,191 African American 1910 population held insurance and the death payments averaged $1,779.45, as suggested in this sample, then those 2,459 individuals (7191 * .342) pumped almost 4.4 million dollars into the Richmond African American community through local funeral homes and related enterprises, if they died in the city. Tracking economic monetary flows of this size may reveal a significantly different interpretation of capital wealth and economic power in the African American community than commonly believed.

Measuring the value of this statistical study by the significant levels achieved is wrong, especially for the ANOVA test. Because the study analyzed average ratios, which can complicate an analysis, and the sample was so small, one must be careful not to make overstatements. Yet, the direction of the analysis does support the arguments by surveys, material culture, and anecdotal material that distinctive cultural-based funeral rituals exist. What this analysis provides is a framework to quantify the cultural differences Americans exhibited in their death customs in the early twentieth century. The research confirms that the African American community placed a higher value on insurance and death benefits than white populations in Richmond and initiates research into the economic consequences of these cultural differences.

Bibliography

Abbott. 1913. "There Are No Dead." *Outlook* (104) 30 August: 979.

Abrahams, Roger D. 1970. *Positively Black*. Englewood Cliffs, New Jersey: Prentice-Hall, Inc.

Adams, Edward C.L., and Robert G. O' Meally. 1987. *Tales of the Congaree*. Chapel Hill, North Carolina: University of North Carolina Press.

Arnold, Adam S. Jr. 1951. The Investments of Seven Negro Life Insurance Companies. Ph.D. Dissertation, University of Wisconsin.

Baker, Houston A. 1984. *Blues, Ideology, and Afro-American Literature: A vernacular theory*. Chicago: University of Chicago Press

Bendann, Efie. 1930. *Death Customs: An Analytical Study of Burial Rites*. New York: Knopf.

Berlin, Ira. 1986. "Time, Space, and the Evolution of Afro American Society." In *The Underside of American History, Fifth Edition, Volume one: To 1877*, edited by Thomas R. Frazier, 83-112. San Diego: Harcourt Brace Jovanovich.

Binga, Anthony J., Sr. 1989. Interview by author, 10 October, Richmond. Tape recording.

Blackwood, Andrew Watterson. 1942. *The Funeral*. Philadelphia: The Westminster Press.

Blassingame, John W. 1979. *The Slave Community*. New York: Oxford University Press.

Bolton, H. Carrington. 1891. "Decoration of Negro Graves in South Carolina" *Journal of American Folk-lore*, 4: 214

Borchert, James. 1980. *Alley Life in Washington: Family, Community, Religion, and Folklife in the City, 1850-1970*. Urbana: University of Illinois Press.

Bowman, Le Roy Edward. 1959. *The American Funeral; A Study in Guilt, Extravagance and Sublimity*. Washington: Public Affairs Office.

Brewer, J. Mason. 1968. *American Negro Folklore*. Chicago: Quadrangle Books.

Brown, Frank C. 1964. *North Carolina Folklore*. Durham: Duke University Press.

Brown, Lawrence N. 1930. The Insurance of American Negro Lives. Master of Business Administration Thesis, University of Pennsylvania.

Brown, Sterling. 1958. "The Spirituals." In *The Book of Negro Folklore*, edited by Langston Hughes and Arna Bontemps. New York: Dodd, Mead and Co.

_____. 1969. "Negro Expressions: Spirituals, Seculars, Ballads, and Work Songs." In *The Making of Black America, Vol. II* by August Meier and Elliot Rudwick. New York: Atheneum.

Radcliffe-Brown, A. R. 1952. "Religion and Society." Essay in *Structure and Function in Primitive Society*. Glencoe, Illinois: The Free Press: 153-177.

Brown, Elsa Barkley. 1989. "Womanist Consciousness: Maggie Lena Walker and The Independent Order of Saint Luke." *Signs: Journal of Women in Culture and Society*, 14(3): 610-633.

Browning, James B. 1937. "The Beginnings of Insurance Enterprise Among Negroes." *The Journal of Negro History*, 22(4): 417-432.

Bureau of the Census. 1975. *Historical Statistics of the United States, Colonial Times to 1970, Bicentennial Edition, Part 1 & 2.* Washington: U. S. Department of Commerce.

Bureau of Consumer Protection. 1978. *Funeral Industry Practices: Final Staff Report to the Federal Trade Commission and Proposed Trade Regulation Rule (16 CFR Part 453).* Washington, D.C.: U.S. Federal Trade Commission.

Butler, John Sibley and Kenneth L. Wilson. 1991. *Entrepreneurial Enclaves in the African American Experience.* Washington, D.C.: Neighborhood Policy Institute.

Carawan, Guy and Candie. 1989. *Ain't You Got a Right to the Tree of Life.* New York: Simon and Schuster, 1966; reprint, Athens: The University of Georgia Press.

Census of Population. 1910. *Thirteenth Census of the United States 1910 Population. Richmond, Virginia.* Washington: National Archives.

Census of Population. 1920. *Thirteenth Census of the United States 1920 Population. Richmond, Virginia.* Washington: National Archives.

Chesson, Michael B. 1981. *Richmond After the War 1865-1890.* Richmond: Virginia State Library.

Childs, John Brown. 1980. *The Political Black Minister.* Boston: G. K. Hall & Co.

Clarke, Erskine. 1979. *Wrestlin' Jacob.* Atlanta: John Knox Press.

Clawson, Mary Ann. 1989. *Constructing Brotherhood: Class, Gender, and*

Fratemalism. Princeton: Princeton University Press.

Cone, James H. 1972. *The Spirituals and the Blues*. New York: The Seabury Press.

Connor, Cynthia. 1989. Sleep On And Take Your Rest: Black Mortuary Behavior on the East Branch of the Cooper River, South Carolina. Master of Arts Thesis, University of South Carolina.

Conroy, Pat. 1972. *The Water Is Wide*. Boston: Houghton Mifflin Company.

Courlander, Harold. 1960. *The Drum and The Hoe*. Berkeley: University of California Press.

Cox, Oliver C. 1950. "Leadership Among Negroes in the United States." In *Studies in Leadership*, edited by Alvin W. Gouldner. New York: Harper & Brothers.

Crocker, Christopher. 1971. "The Southern Way of Death." *In The Not So Solid South*, edited by J. Kenneth Morland, 114-129. Athens: University of Georgia Press.

Curtin, Philip D. 1969. *The Atlantic Slave Trade; a Census*. Madison: University of Wisconsin Press.

Davis, Edwin Adams and William R. Hogan. 1973. *The Barber of Natchez*. Baton Rouge: Louisiana State University Press, 1954; reprint.

Davis, Susan G. 1986. *Parades and Power: Street Theatre in Nineteenth-Century Philadelphia*. Philadelphia: Temple University Press.

Dyson, Reginald. 1989. Interview by author, 17 October, Richmond. Tape recording.

_____. 1989. Interview by author, 28 November 1989, Richmond. Tape recording.

Dixwell, John. 1908. "Mourning Customs of Negroes." *Journal of American Folk-lore* 21: 365.

Douglas, Mary. 1966. *Purity and Danger: an analysis of concepts of pollution and taboo*. London: Routledge & K. Paul.

_____. 1973. *Natural Symbols: Explorations in Cosmology*. London: Barrie and Rockliff. 1970; 2nd edition, London: Barrie and Jenkins.

_____. 1975. *Implicit Meanings*. London: Routledge and Kegan Paul.

_____. 1979. *Cultural Bias*. London: Royal Anthropological Institute.

Dowd, Quincy L. 1921. *Funeral Management and Costs: A World Survey of Burial and Cremation*. Chicago: University of Chicago Press.

Drake, St.Clair and Horace Cayton. 1963. "Urban Burying Leagues." In *The Book of Negro Folklore*, edited by Langston Hughes and Arna Bontemps. Dodd Mead, 1958; reprint.

Du Bois, W.E.B. 1899. *The Philadelphia Negro: A Social Study*. Philadelphia: Publications of the University of Pennsylvania. Series in political economy and public law, Number 14.

_____. 1907. *Economic Co-operation Among American Negroes*. Atlanta: Atlanta University Publications, Number 12.

_____. 1908. *The Negro in Business*. Atlanta: Atlanta University Publications, Number 4.

_____. 1990. *The Souls of Black Folk*. New York: Vintage Books, 1903; reprint.

Durkheim, Emile. 1915. *The Elementary Forms of the Religious Life*. New York: Free Press.

Dye, Thomas R. 1973. *Politics in States and Communities*. Englewood Cliffs: Prentice-Hall, Inc.

Earle, Alice M. 1893. *Customs and Fashions in Old New England*. New York: Charles Scribner's Sons.

Epstein, Dena J. 1977. *Sinful Tunes and Spirituals*. Urbana: University of Illinois Press.

Farrell, James J. 1980. *Inventing the American Way of Death, 1830-1920*. Philadelphia: Temple Press.

Fauset, Arthur H. 1944. *Black Gods of the Metropolis*. Philadelphia: University of Pennsylvania Press.

Federal Trade Commission. 1977. *Report of the Presiding Officer on Proposed Trade Regulation Rule Concerning Funeral Industry Practices*. Washington, D.C.: The Commission.

Fenn, Elizabeth A. 1989. "Honoring the Ancestors: Kongo-American Graves in the American South. In *The Last Miles of the Way: African American Homegoing Traditions, 1890-Present*, edited by Elaine Nichols, 44-50. Columbia, S.C.: Commissioners of the South Carolina State Museum.

Fishbane, Simcha. 1989. "Jewish Mourning Rites-A Process of Resocialization." *Anthropologica*. XXXI: 65-84.

Fletcher, Linda Pickthorne. 1970. *The Negro in the Insurance Industry*. Philadelphia: University of Pennsylvania Press.

Folly, Dennis W. 1980. "You Preach your Funeral While you Living": Death in Afro-American Folklore. Master of Arts Thesis, University of California, Berkeley.

Frazier, E. Franklin. 1939. *The Negro Family in the United States*. Chicago: University of Chicago Press.

Fulton, Robert. 1961. "The Clergyman and the Funeral Director: A Study in Role Conflict." *Social Forces* 39 (May): 317-23.

_____. 1967. *A Compilation of Studies of Attitudes toward Death, Funerals, and Funeral Directors*. Minneapolis: National Funeral Directors Association.

Galante, Frank. 1976. "The Italian Family: How it Deals with Acute Grief and the Funeral."*In Acute Grief and The Funeral*, edited by Vanderlyn R. Pine. Springfield: Charles C. Thomas.

Gardner, Thomas J. 1958. Problems in the Development of Financial Institutions Among Negroes: Historical Development, Current Trends, and The Future in Business. Doctor of Business Administration Dissertation, New York University.

Gatewood, Willard B. 1990. *Aristocrats of Color*. Bloomington: Indiana University Press.

Gavins, Raymond. 1977. *The Perils and Prospects of Southern Black Leadership*. Durham, N.C.: Duke University Press.

Gebhart, John C. 1928. *Funeral Costs: What they Average. Are they too high? Can they be reduced?* New York-London:Putnam.

Genovese, Eugene D. 1976. *Roll, Jordan, Roll*. New York: Pantheon Books 1974; reprint, New York: First Vintage Books.

Georgia Writers' Project, Savannah Unit, Work Projects Administration. 1973. *Drums and Shadows*. Athens: University of Georgia Press, 1940; reprint, Westport: Greenwood Press.

Glave, E. J. 1891. "Fetishism in Congo Land." *The Century Magazine* 41.

Goldston, Maude P. 1962. An Analysis of Life Insurance Programs of Selected Families in Durham, North Carolina. Master of Science Thesis, North Carolina College at Durham.

Goody, Jack. 1962. *Death Property and the Ancestors: A Study of the Mortuary Customs of the Lodagaa of West Africa*. Stanford: Stanford University.

Gorer, Geoffrey. 1987. *Death, Grief, and Mourning in Contemporary Britain*. London: The Cresset Press, 1965; reprint, Salem, New Hampshire: Ayer Company Publishers, Inc.

Habenstein, Robert W. & William M. Lamers. 1956. *The History of American Funeral Directing*. Milwaukee: Bulfin Printer, 1955; reprint.

_____. 1963. *Funeral Customs The World Over*. Milwaukee: Bulfin Printer.

Hacker, Andrew. 1992. *Two Nations: Black and White, Separate, Hostile, Unequal*. New York: Charles Scribner's Sons.

Hall, Robert L. 1990. "African religious Retentions in Florida." In *Africanisms in American Culture*, edited by Joseph E. Holloway.

Bloomington and Indianapolis: Indiana University Press.

Handler, Jerome S. and Frederick W. Lange. 1978. *Plantation Slavery in Barbados*. Cambridge: Harvard University Press.

Harmer, Ruth M. 1963. *The High Cost of Dying*. New York:Collier Books.

Harmon, J.H., Arnett G. Lindsay and Carter G. Woodson. 1929. *The Negro as Businessman*. Washington: Assoc. for the Study of Negro Life and History, Inc.

Harrison, April K. 1982. Social Dimensions of Mortuary Practices of Late Nineteenth-Century Black Atlantans. Honors Thesis, Georgia State University.

Hatcher, William E. 1908. *John Jasper*. New York: Fleming H. Revell Company.

Henderson, Alexa B. 1987. "Heman E. Perry and Black Enterprise in Atlanta, 1908-1925," *Business History Review* 61(2) (Summer): 216-242.

Herskovits, Melville. 1941. *The Myth of the Negro Past*. New York: Harper & Brothers.

Hertz, R. 1960. "A Contribution to the Study of the Collective Representation of Death [1907]." In *Death and the Right Hand*, translation by Rodney and Claudia Needham. Glencoe, Illinois: The Free Press.

Hill, Arthur C. 1976. "The Black Funeral Director in Minnesota." Sociology course 8956-8957, University of Minnesota.

_____. 1983. "The Impact of Urbanism on Death and Dying among Black People in a Rural Community in Middle Tennessee." *Omega* 14.2: 171-185.

Hoffman, Frederick L. 1919. "Paper Burials and the Interment of the Dead in Large Cities." An address read at the National Conference of Social Work, Atlantic City, 4 June.

Hohenschuh, W.P. 1900. *The Modern Funeral: Its Management*. Chicago: Trade Periodical Company.

Holloway, Joseph E., editor. 1990. *Africanisms in American Culture*. Bloomington and Indianapolis: Indiana University Press.

Hughes, Langston & Arna Bontemps, editors. 1959. *The Book of Negro Folklore*. New York: Dodd, Mead & Company.

Huntington, Richard and Peter Metcalf. 1980. *Celebrations of Death*. Cambridge: Cambridge University Press, 1979; reprint.

Hulvey, Charles N. and William H. Wandel. 1929. *Life Insurance in Virginia*. Charlottesville, Va.: The Institute for Research in the

Social Sciences, University of Virginia.

Ingersoll, Ernest. "Decoration of Negro Graves." 1892. *Journal of American Folk-lore* 5: 68-69.

Irion, Paul E. 1954. *The Funeral and the Mourners*. New York: Abingdon Press.

Jackson, Bruce, editor. 1967. *The Negro and His Folklore in Nineteenth-Century Periodicals*. Austin: University of Texas Press.

Jackson, George Pullen. 1933. *White Spirituals in the Southern Uplands*. Chapel Hill: The University of North Carolina Press.

Jackson, Maurice. 1972. "The Black Experience with Death: A Brief Analysis Through Black Writings." *Omega* 3.3 (August): 203-209.

Janzen, John M. and Wyatat MacGaffey. 1974. *An Anthology of Kongo Religion:Primary Texts from Flower Zaire*. Lawrence: University of Kansas Press.

Johnson, Charles S. 1934. *Shadow of the Plantation*. Chicago: The University of Chicago Press.

Joyner, Charles. 1984. *Down by the Riverside*. Urbana: University of Illinois Press.

Kalish, Richard A. 1968. "Life and Death: Dividing the Indivisible," *Social Science and Medicine*. Great Britain: Pergamon Press. 2: 249-259.

_____, Editor. 1980. *Death and Dying: Views From Many Cultures*. Farmingdale,N.Y.:Baywood Publishing Company, Inc.

_____ and David K. Reynolds. 1981. *Death and Ethnicity:A Psychocultural Study*. Ethel Percy Andrus Gerontology Center, 1976; reprint, Farmingdale: Baywood Publishing Company, Inc.

Kennedy, Williams., Jr. 1970. *The North Carolina Mutual Story: A Symbol of Progress, 1898-1970*. Durham: North Carolina Mutual Life Insurance.

Kephart, William M. 1950. "Status after Death," *American Sociological Review*. 15 (October): 635-643.

Kenzer, Robert C. 1989. "The Black Businessman in the Postwar South: North Carolina, 1865-1880," *Business History Review* 63(1) (Spring): 61-87.

Kertzer, David. 1988. *Ritual, Politics, and Power*. New Haven: Yale University Press.

Kinzer, Robert H. and Edward Sagarin. 1950. *The Negro in American Business: The Conflict between Separatism and Integration*. New York: Greenberg.

Kip, Richard De Raismes. 1953. *Fraternal Life Insurance In America*.

Philadelphia: College Offset Press.

Krepps, Karen L. 1990. *Black Mortuary Practices in Southeast Michigan.* Ph.D. Dissertation, Wayne State University.

Krieger, William M. 1951. *Successful Funeral Service Management.* Englewood Cliffs: Prentice-Hall, Inc.

Krieger, Wilber. 1954. "Facts help Interpret Funeral Service", *Casket and Sunnyside.* LXXXIV, 9(September).

Kulikoff, Allan. 1977. "A "Prolifick" People: Black Population Growth in the Chesapeake Colonies, 1700-1790." *Southern Studies*, (Winter): 391-427.

Levine, Lawrence W. 1977. *Black Culture and Black Consciousness.* New York: Oxford University Press.

Lewin, Kurt. 1950. "The Problem of Minority Leadership." In *Studies in Leadership*, edited by Alvin W. Gouldner. New York: Harper & Brothers.

Lovell, John Jr. 1969. "The Social Implications of the Negro Spiritual." In *The Social Implications of Early Negro Music in the United States*, edited by Bernard Katz. New York: Arno Press, 1939; reprint.

_____. 1972. *Black Song.* New York: MacMillian Company.

Lunceford, Ron and Judy Lunceford. 1976. *Attitudes on Death and Dying: A Cross-cultural View.* Los Alamitos, Ca.: Hwong Publishing Co.

Margolis, Otto S., Howard C. Raether, Austin H. Kutscher, Robert J. Volk, Ivan K. Goldberg, and Daniel J. Cherico, editors. 1975. *Grief and the Meaning of the Funeral.* New York: MSS Information Corporation.

Marvick, Dwaine. 1965. "The Political Socialization of the American Negro." *Annals of the American Academy of Political and Social Science*, 361 (September): 123. Quoted in Thomas R. Dye. *Politics in States and Communities.* 405. Englewood Cliffs: Prentice-Hall, Inc., 1973.

Masamba, Jean and Richard Kalish. 1976. "Death and Bereavement: The Role of the Black Church." *Omega* 7.1 : 23-24.

Mays, B. and J. Nicholson. 1933. *The Negro Church.* New York: Institute of Social & Religious Research.

Mbiti, John S. 1975. *Introduction to African Religion.* New York: Praeger Publishers.

McDill, McCown & Gassman. 1952. *Daddy Was An Undertaker.* New York:Vantage Press.

McDonald, Morris J. 1973. "The Management of Grief: A Study of Black

Funeral Practices." *Omega* 4.2 : 139-148.

McGee, Charlotte L. and Phyllis P. Scoby. 1981. A Comparative Study of Current Practices of Secular Mortuary Chapel Funeral Services of Black and White Families. Master of Arts Thesis, California State University.

Meeker, Edward. 1977. "Freedom, Economic Opportunity and Fertility: Black Americans 1860-1910." *Economic Inquiry*. 15(3) (July):397-412.

Menard, Russell R. 1975. "The Maryland Slave Population, 1658 to 1730: A Demographic Profile of Blacks in Four Countries." *William and Mary Quarterly*. 32 (January): 29-54.

Metzger, Clarence B. 1926. *Contributions of Life Insurance Research to the Estate Problem, 1925. National Wealth and Income*. Washington, D.C.: Federal Trade Commission.

Miller, Joseph C. 1988. *Way of Death: Merchant Capitalism and the Angolan Slave Trade, 1730-1830*. London: Currey Press.

Mitford, Jessica. 1963. *The American Way of Death*. New York: Simon and Schuster.

Moore, Joan. 1980. "The Death Culture of Mexico and Mexican Americans." In *Death and Dying: Views From Many Cultures*, edited by Richard A. Kalish. Farmingdale,N.Y.:Baywood Publishing Company, Inc.

Moses, Wilson Jeremiah. 1978. *The Golden Age of Black Nationalism: 1850-1925*. Hamden, Connecticut: Archon Book.

Nelson, Hart. editor. 1971. *The Black Church in America*. New York:Basic Book.

Nichols, Elaine. editor. 1989. *The Last Miles of the Way: African American Homegoing Traditions, 1890-Present*. Columbia, S.C.: Commissioners of the South Carolina State Museum.

Oak, Vishnu Vitthal. 1949. *The Negro's Adventure in General Business*. The Negro Entrepreneur Series. Yellow Springs, Ohio:Antioch Press.

Oliver, Paul. 1960. *Blues Fell This Morning*. Cambridge: Cambridge University Press.

Oster, Harry. 1969. *Living Country Blues*. Detroit: Folklore Associates.

Park, Robert E. 1919. "The Conflict and Fusion of Culture," *Journal of Negro History* IV.

Paz, Octavio. 1961. *The Labyrinth of Solitude: life and thought in Mexico*. New York: Grove Press.

Pierce, Joseph A. 1971. "The Evolution of Negro Business." In *Black*

186 African American Entrepreneurship in Richmond

Business Enterprise: Historical and Contemporary Perspectives, edited by Ronald W. Bailey. New York: Basic Books, Inc.

Pine, Vanderlyn R. 1975. *Caretaker of the Dead: The American Funeral Director*. New York: Irvington Publishers, Inc.

_____, Austin H. Kutscher, David Peretz, Robert C. Slater, Robert DeBellis, Robert J. Volk, and Daniel J. Cherico, editors. 1976. *Acute Grief and The Funeral*. Springfield: Charles C. Thomas.

_____, Vanderlyn R. and Derek L. Phillips. 1970. "The Cost of Dying: A Sociological Analysis of Funeral Expenditures." *Social Problems* 17 (Winter):405-17.

Pipes, William H. 1951. *Say Amen, Brother!* Westport: Negro Universities Press.

Plater, Michael A. 1993. R. C. Scott: A History of African American Entrepreneurship in Richmond, 1890-1940. Ph.D. Dissertation, College of William and Mary.

Powdermaker, Hortense. 1968. *After Freedom*. 1939; reissued, New York: Russell & Russell.

Puckett, Newbell W. 1969. *The Magic and Folk Beliefs of the Southern Negro*. Chapel Hill: University of North Carolina Press, 1926; reprint, New York: Dover Publications, Inc.

Puth, Robert. 1969. "Supreme Life :The History of a Negro Life Insurance Company 1919-1962." *Business of Historical Review*. 43(1): 1-20.

Rachleff, Peter J. 1984. *Black Labor in the South: Richmond, Virginia, 1865-1890*. Philadelphia: Temple University Press.

Rawick, George P. 1972. *The American Slave*. Westport: Greenwood Publishing Company.

Reid, Ira De A. 1968. *The Negro Immigrant*. New York: Columbia University Press, 1939; reprint, New York: AMS press.

Richmond Planet. 4 January 1890-7 December 1929.

Roediger, David R. 1981. "And Die in Dixie, Funerals, Death and Heaven in the Slave Community." *Massachusetts Review* 22: 163-168.

Rosenblatt, Paul C., R. Patricia Walsh, and Douglass A. Jackson. 1976. *Grief and Mourning in Cross Cultural Perspective*. New Haven: HRAF Press.

Schwartz, Barry. 1991. "Mourning and the Making of a Sacred Symbol: Durkheim and the Lincoln Assassination," *Social Forces* 70(2) (December): 343-364.

Schweninger, Loren. 1989. "Black-Owned Businesses in the South, 1790-1880," *Business History Review*. 63(1) (Spring): 22-60.

Scott, Robert Crafton, Sr. 1953-1957. An Autobiography dictated to Anthony J. Binga, Sr.

Sisk, Glenn. 1959. "Funeral Customs in the Alabama Black Belt," *Southern Folklore Quarterly* 23: 169-171.

Silver, Christopher. 1984. *Twentieth-Century Richmond*. Knoxville: University of Tennessee Press.

Sobel, Mechal. 1987. *The World They Made Together: Black and White Values in Eighteenth-Century Virginia*. Princeton: Princeton University Press.

_____, 1988. *Trabelin' On, The Slave Journey to an Afro-Baptist Faith*. Princeton: Princeton University Press.

Southern Aid Messenger. 1908. Annual publication of The Southern Aid Society of Virginia.

Southern Workman. 1897. "Beliefs and Customs Connected With Death and Burial." 26: 18-19.

Stannard, David E., editor. 1975. *Death In America*. Philadelphia: University of Pennsylvania Press.

Steele, Joshua. 1978. Letters of Philo-Xylon, 1787-88. In *Mitigation of slavery in two parts*, by William Dickson. London, 1814, 65-142. Quoted in Handler, Jerome S. and Frederick W. Lange. *Plantation Slavery in Barbados*. Cambridge: Harvard University Press.

Stuart, M.S. 1969. *An Economic Detour: A History of Life Insurance in the lives of American Negroes*. New York: McGrath Publishing Company, 1940; reprint.

Sudnow, David. 1967. *Passing On*. Englewood Cliffs: Prentice Hall, Inc.

Thompson, Robert F. 1983. *Flash of the Spirit*. New York: Random House.

Thompson, Robert and Joseph Cornet. 1981. *The Four Moments of the Sun: Kongo Art in Two Worlds*. Washington D.C.: National Gallery of Art.

Toynbee, Arnold A., Keith Mant, Nina Smart, John Hinton, Simon Yudkin, Eric Rhode, Rosalin Heywood, and H.H. Price. 1968. *Man's Concern With Death*. St. Louis: McGraw-Hill.

Trent, W. J. Jr. 1932. Development of Negro Life Insurance Enterprises. Master of Business Administration Thesis, University of Pennsylvania.

Turner, Victor. 1969. *The Ritual Process: Structure and Anti-Structure*. Ithaca, New York: Cornell University Press.

_____. 1974. *Dramas, Fields and Metaphors: Symbolic Action in Human Society*. Ithaca: Cornell University Press.

Twining, Mary A. 1977. An Examination of African Retentions in the Folk Culture of the South Carolina and Georgia Sea Islands. Ph.D. Dissertation, Indiana University.

Vernon, G.M. 1970. *Sociology of Death*. New York: The Ronald Press Company.

Wade, Richard C. 1964. *Slavery in the Cities*. New York: Oxford University Press.

Waite, E. Emerson,Jr. 1940. Social Factors in Negro Business Enterprise. Master of Arts Thesis, Duke University.

Walker, Juliet E. K. 1986. "Racism, Slavery, and Free Enterprise: Black Entrepreneurship in the United States before the Civil War," *Business History Review* 60(3) (Autumn): 343-382.

Washington, Booker T. 1907. *The Negro in Business*. Boston: Hertel, Jenkins & Co.

Washington Post. 30 April 1993.

Weare, Walter B. 1973. *Black Business in the New South: A Social History of the North Carolina Mutual Life Insurance Company*. Urbana: University of Illinois Press.

Weeks, John H. 1914. *Among the Primitive Bakongo*. London: Seeley, Service & Co.

White, Newman. 1928. *American Negro Folk Songs*. Hatboro, Pennsylvania: Folklore Associates, Inc.

Wilson, K. and W. Martin. 1982. "Ethnic Enclaves: A Comparison of the Cuban and Black Economies in Miami," *American Journal of Sociology*. 88: 135-160.

Wilson, K. and A. Portes. 1980. "Immigrant Enclaves: An Analysis of the Labor Market Experience of Cubans in Miami," *American Journal of Sociology*. 86: 295-319

Woodson, Carter. 1969. *The Negro Professional Man and the Community*. New York: Negro Universities Press 1934, reprint.

Index

African Methodist Episcopal, 110
Ashe, Arthur, xiii
Atlantic Slave Trade, 90

Bantu culture, 90, 98
Bliley, Joseph ,9
Bradshaw, Booker Talmadge 148
Brown Fellowship Society, 109, 119
Brown, Morris, 119
Browne, William W. , 140

Children's funerals, 52, 56, 79
Coffin warehouses, 41
Commercial Bank, 29
Consolidated Bank and Trust Company, 29
Courting ritual, 7
Crane, Breed & Co., 42

Demographic changes, 49
Du Bois, W.E.B. xviii, xix, 119, 163

Early American Burials, 41
Embalming
  Hygienic advantages, 25
  Civil War, 23, 44
  Freezing method, 23
Eenclave theory, xiv, xx, xxi
Epidemic of influenza, 27
Ethnic-Based Death Rituals, 59
Evergreen Cemetery, xiii, 15

Federal Trade Commission, 60, 61, 123, 126

Fisk Metallic Coffin, 42
Fraternal orders, 9, 30, 133, 134
Free African Society, 119
Funeral Director Profession, 46

Government Regulations, 60
  Embalming procedures, 48
  State embalming requirements, 52
  Transporting bodies, 48
Grand Fountain of the United Order of True Reformers, 142, 145, 146
Gunn, Julien M., 33, 35, 163

Hayes, C.P., 31
Hewin, J. Thomas, 329
Humane Brotherhood, 109

Independent Order of Saint Luke, 5
Insurance Enterprises
  Church Relief Societies, 130
  Fraternal Benefit Societies, 131
  Insurance Companies, 144

Jackson Ward, 9
Johnson. W. I., 3
Johnson's Auditorium, 16

Knights of Pythias, 13

Market Structure, 49
Mechanics Savings Bank, 26
Metropolitan Life Insurance
    Company, 61
Mitchell, John, xiii, 13, 26
Mourning Rituals, 84

NAACP, xx
National Associations of
    Funeral Directors, 31
National Benefit Life Insurance
    Company , 35
National Funeral Directors
    Association, 48
National Negro Funeral
    Directors Association,
    48
National Selected Morticians,
    56
Negro Business League, 13
Neighborhood Chapel, 32, 37

Parades, 134
Pauper burial, 118
Planet, The Richmond xxi
Price's hall, 12
Prudential Insurance Company,
    134

Railroad excursions, 136
Reid, Dr. Leon A., 29
Richmond Beneficial Insurance
    Company, 29
Richmond Funeral Directors
    Association, 32
Richmond Hospital Association,
    13
Richmond Welfare League, 16
Robinson, Bill "Bojangles", 33,
    36, 148

Robinson, Spottswood W., 29
Russell, Charles T., 29, 32

Seaside Park, 14, 134
Second Street Bank, 29
Slave Funerals, 107
Songs
    blues, 112, 115
    spirituals, 112
Southern Aid Insurance, 15, 29,
    145, 148
Spanish-American War, 19

St. Luke Emporium, 5
St. Luke Penny Savings Bank,
    29
Stock market crash, 34
Stokes, Ora B., 15

Turner, Anthony H., 32

Vesey, Denmark, 119
Virginia Mutual Benefit Life
    Insurance Company,
    35, 149, 163

Walker, Maggie, xiii, 5, 29
Washington, Booker T., xviii,
    xx, 117, 163
Woodland Cemetery, xiii

Michael Andre' Plater

The author was born in Washington, D.C. on April 24, 1956. He graduated from The Phillips Exeter Academy in January 1974. After spending his junior year on a New York Urban Fellowship, he received his A.B. in Economics from Harvard University in June 1979. In December 1982, the author earned an MBA from The Wharton School, University of Pennsylvania with a concentration in Entrepreneurship.

After receiving his MBA, the author spent four years working in the Strategic Planning division of Standard Oil of Ohio (BP America). He left this organization in 1986 to begin doctoral studies in American Studies at William and Mary, while serving as a member of the Business School faculty. The author received his Ph.D. in 1993 and joined the faculty of the College of Business at the University of Florida. He currently teaches courses on Business Policy, Entrepreneurship and Business History at the University of Florida.

For Product Safety Concerns and Information please contact our
EU representative GPSR@taylorandfrancis.com Taylor & Francis
Verlag GmbH, Kaufingerstraße 24, 80331 München, Germany